HULDRYCH ZWINGLI

HULDRYCH ZWINGLI

His Life and Work

ULRICH GÄBLER

Translated by Ruth C. L. Gritsch

T. & T. CLARK LTD.
59 GEORGE STREET, EDINBURGH

English Translation Copyright © Fortress Press, 1986.

Originally published under the title
Huldrych Zwingli: Leben und Werk
by C. M. Beck, Munich, 1983.

Printed in the U.K. by Billing & Sons, Worcester,

for

T. & T. CLARK LTD., EDINBURGH.

First printed in the U.K. 1987.

British Library Cataloguing in Publication Data

Gäbler, Ulrich
Huldrych Zwingli: his life and work.
1. Zwingli, Ulrich   2. Reformation—Switzerland—Biography
I. Title   II. Huldrych Zwingli, *English*
270.6'092'4   BR345

ISBN 0–567–09449–9

Dedicated to
Christa
Florian, Nikolaus, Elisabeth

CONTENTS

PREFACE

At stake in this introduction to Huldrych Zwingli's life and work is not a comprehensive treatment but a sketch of the basic theme, a survey of the research, and an aid to further research. In view of the diversity of material, certain questions and problems could only be dealt with summarily and paradigmatically. Thus it was not always possible to give detailed reasons for my own view. Nevertheless, neither the selection necessary nor the brevity required should impair intelligibility and balance.

A particular problem was thorough study and citation of the literature. Since the Zwingli bibliography is quite accessible, literary references have been reduced to a minimum. The bibliographical supplements to each chapter are primarily intended to offer starting points to intensified research, and also point to the basic treatises on which my presentation is based. I have used the publications listed in chapter XI throughout, especially the two comprehensive presentations by Gottfried W. Locher. The abbreviations have been explained either in chapter XI or in the bibliography of the appropriate chapter.

In working on this manuscript I have had frequent help. I thank Prof. Dr. Fritz Büsser in Zurich for his friendly permission to study the galleys of volume VI/III of the critical Zwingli edition. Dr. Joachim Rogge of East Berlin made available to me the manuscript of his Zwingli section in the series "Church History in Individual Presentations" (East Berlin, 1978–   ); publication of this important and original contribution is expected before the end of this year. I owe special thanks to Dr. Matthias Senn of Zurich, who looked through my manuscript, improved the style, helped to proofread, and thus kept me from making several serious blunders. My colleague here, Prof. Cornelius Augustijn, was my critical partner in dialogue last year. I profited greatly from his knowledge as well as from his way — rooted in Dutch tradition — of dealing with history. I hope to pass some of this on to the reader. The participants in a seminar on Zwingli, co-chaired with Augustijn in the winter semester of 1982, increased my insight into the complexity of the problems. I also enjoyed the particular support of three students: Arjen Breukelaar devoted himself to bibliographical investigations; Ewout Broekema made valuable contributions by checking quotations and footnotes; and Annerien Groenendijk helped me read the galleys and arrange the indexes. I thank all three for their unflagging helpfulness. I conclude this manuscript with a feeling of gratitude to those who accompanied my fifteen years in Zurich. The dedication names my closest companions.

Ulrich Gäbler

Amsterdam, February 1983

I
THE ENVIRONMENT

1. The Legal Structure of the
Swiss Confederation

In Huldrych Zwingli's time, the Swiss Confederation encompassed about the same geographical territory as it does today. Nor have the interior boundaries of the individual territories changed much. Their relationship to each other was, however, changed radically by the establishment of the Federal Republic at the beginning of the nineteenth century, because at that time every canton was granted the same rights. In the sixteenth century, the Confederation consisted of three groups of districts with differing degrees of sovereignty: the thirteen Independent States, the Affiliated States, and the Common Lordships.

The so-called original cantons (*Urkantone*) of Schwyz, Uri, and Unterwalden, which had formed a league in 1291, formed special alliances with ten more territories until 1513. Lucerne, Zurich, Zug, Glarus, and Bern attained full membership. They, along with the original cantons, formed the eight Ancient States. Freiburg, Solothurn, Basel, Schaffhausen, and Appenzell were added later. Accession to the Confederation did not restrict the autonomy of its members constitutionally, since the member states could conduct their own domestic and foreign affairs. The only thing they had to guard against was forming a new alliance conflicting with their obligations to co-confederates. To this extent, the individual state's freedom of movement in foreign affairs was checked only when the interests of the Confederation as a whole were at stake. This formed the basis of conflict at the time of the Reformation, since the various confessional camps gave contradictory answers to the question of what best served the Confederation.

Since there was neither a permanent parliament nor a central authority, ambassadors from the states met only when one of the federation members demanded it, or when periodically recurring affairs required settlement. No state was required to send an ambassador to such a Diet. Nor could those assembled there arrive at any binding dispositions, although almost no state would refuse to enforce a unanimous resolution of the Diet. In any case, the Diet had no means of coercion available to it when faced with the opposition of a minority. If there was a fundamental disagreement, the Diet was adjourned to give ambassadors the opportunity to receive new instructions from their governments.

The eight Ancient States administered Common Lordships or bailiwicks like the county of Baden, the free communities, the landgravate of Thurgau, and the Rhine valley. These districts had for the most part been annexed through conquest by all or by several states, which were now responsible for administering them. The respective states authorized to do so governed through alternately appointed guardians who were obliged to report and render accounts annually. Administering these twenty vassal districts by means of regular consultations and enactment of regulations created "an important cement to bind the Confederation together."[1] In contradistinction to the Diet, majority rule was in force. In case of disagreement among the ruling states, therefore, the minority had no possibility of thwarting or even delaying the enforcement of a regulation.

The third group of Confederates, the Affiliated States, did not participate in the administration of vassal districts; some of them were even partially dependent on the thirteen Independent States. They therefore had less influence on the policies of the Confederation. Among the most important Affiliated States were the ducal abbey of St. Gallen, the city of St. Gallen, Mühlhausen, Rottweil, Biel, Graubünden, and the Valais.

The constitutional structure of the Confederation — of which only the basic elements are described above — which in practice proved to be a variegated mesh of interdependencies, determined the course of Reformation history in Switzerland. Any essential change at all could be initiated only by one of the thirteen Independent States, which would then have to win others to its cause without using coercion. Each state decided religious matters freely in its own territory. Difficulties inevitably arose in the Common Lordships when the states governing them belonged to differing camps in confessional controversies, and when each side tried, through a loyal guardian, to have its own views adopted.

The political and legal systems of the individual confederates presented a scene of almost incalculable variety. If the rural districts (Uri, Schwyz, Unterwalden, Glarus, and Appenzell) could be called peasant democracies, substantial differences among the inhabitants persisted in city-states like Bern and Zurich, since their rural population was just as unable to exert any influence on government affairs as the urban proletariat. The cities' sovereignty turned peasants into second-class citizens, thus providing material for constant controversy. Nevertheless, the rural communities of Zurich dependent on the city did succeed, by the end of the fifteenth century, in achieving a modest amount of local self-government. They won the right to nominate officials to positions at the lowest level of government (subguardians). One could no longer simply set alien masters over the vassal districts.

Thus all Swiss states had a share of sovereign rights over other Confederate citizens, either in the Confederate league or in their own territory. They were not offended by the fact that in their own federation — which they had once formed precisely to combat this kind of sovereign rights — 70 percent of all inhabitants were vassals with inferior rights.

In the fifteenth century, there was so much competition among the Confederate States to acquire new territory that Zurich even went to war against its neighbor Schwyz in 1443. But the other Confederates immediately came to the aid of this small federation member, and Zurich suffered a devastating defeat. This so-called Old Zurich War would, in the sixteenth century, provide Zurich's opponents with the welcome argument that Zurich had always violated both the spirit and the letter of Confederate agreements. The conflict over new acquisition of territories was finally resolved in 1481 by a solemn treaty in which each side promised to respect the other's vassal district and to protect the Common Lordships.

Aside from the intricate legal system, the situation was further complicated by the fact that there were significant differences in political power among the thirteen Independent States. One item of proof is the population figures, although very few districts provided relatively accurate figures: if one counts a total population of 800,000 in the Confederation in the middle of the sixteenth century, then the two territories of Zurich and Bern alone accounted for more than one-fourth; and these two states did in fact have both economic and political control in the late Middle Ages.

2. The Confederation at the Beginning of the Sixteenth Century

The wars against the House of Hapsburg/Austria in the fourteenth century were still marked by the resistance of citizens and peasants to an expanding princely power. The victories of Morgarten (1315), Sempach (1386), and Näfels (1388) were therefore registered in Confederate national consciousness as the triumph of freedom-loving people over oppressive tyrants. Zwingli would later remember these victories with pride.

The wars of the fifteenth century were another matter. Exploiting the unstable situation following the Old Zurich War, a huge French army invaded Confederate soil in the vicinity of Basel, but was forced to retreat in the face of a self-sacrificial counterattack. This example of Confederate military prowess so impressed France that thirty years later, when the Confederation was in danger of succumbing to Burgundy's lust for power, it offered the Confederation rear cover, thus making their victory against Charles the Bold of Burgundy possible.

This association with France proved to be particularly durable, and for centuries the foreign policy of Switzerland was determined by its relationship to France. On the Swiss side, Bern in particular maintained relations with its western neighbor.

Relations with the Hapsburgs and the Holy Roman Empire were clarified toward the end of the fifteenth century, when the members of the Confederation rejected the 1495 reform resolutions of the Diet of Worms. The sovereignty of princes (*fürstenherrschaft*) that they thought prevailed in the empire was a constant and extreme offense to them. By this time, the Confederation's supraregional legal system was already so well developed, and their political relationships so firmly established, that their bonds to the empire seemed superfluous. In addition, they now eliminated the last of the Austrian royal privileges in Graubünden, and, under the leadership of Zurich, successfully repulsed an intervention by the empire's troops. Emperor Maximilian I was forced to end this so-called Swabian War with the Peace of Basel in 1499, and to admit that the Confederate States were released from all obligations to the empire. Switzerland had in fact seceded from the empire and had become independent. Whether a full constitutional separation occurred at this time, or whether that did not occur until the Westphalian Peace of 1648, is being debated by researchers. The matter can be dropped at this point.

Thus during the fourteenth and fifteenth centuries, the Confederation defended itself successfully on the battlefield against the claims to sovereignty of its neighbors while at the same time expanding and securing its own territory, and it won for itself a place as equal partner in the configuration of European nations.

With regard to foreign policy, the Confederation also found it necessary to take sides in the territorial conflicts of neighboring great powers. At this time, France and the pope — who was the secular ruler of a part of the Apennine peninsula — were fighting over the Duchy of Milan. Milan was located in the Confederation's immediate sphere of influence, because from here was controlled the economically essential southern leg of the Alpine passages to Italy. Remembering the Burgundian Wars, the Confederates first fought on the side of the French, but then, in 1510, switched to the pope's side. At first they even drove French troops out of northern Italy; but in 1515 they suffered a defeat near Mariguano (south of Milan, today called Melegnano), which had a sobering military as well as political effect. With the exception of Zurich, the mood of the Confederation changed, and the partisans of France again gained the upper hand. On May 5, 1521, King Francis I was granted the right to recruit troops in Switzerland.

These relationships with other countries had exceedingly far-reaching political, economic, and social consequences, because they established the so-called pension arrangement on which later Swiss religious factions would pass controversial judgments. Whereas feudal territorial nations like France were almost incapable of recruiting infantry troops of their own, the war-proficient members of the Confederation suffered from overpopulation, which made for an increasing paucity of domestic possibilities for employment. The authorities saw in military service abroad a chance to guide population growth on the one hand, and, on the other hand, to rid themselves of seething social problems with the lowest classes in both city and countryside. But above all, they saw it as a comfortable way to get richer. In addition to particulars regarding pay and length of service, the agreements also contained provisions to compensate the Confederate States. Furthermore, foreign powers paid large sums to individual influential politicians to make them tractable to their interests. Thus factions arose in Switzerland that competed for support for France, the pope, Venice, Savoy, or Austria. These foreign payments, called "pensions" because of the annual settlement of accounts, enabled the leading citizens of Switzerland to live in a style in no way inferior to the standards of the upper classes in other countries.

The pension arrangement came under attack from several sides. Some, out of patriotism, pilloried military service in foreign armies and objected to foreign influence on Switzerland in general; others castigated the moral corruption and the increasing luxury created by this easy money, which only gave rise to inflation. Patriotic moralists demanded a return to the simple life of their ancestors. After their first nationalistic enthusiasm, Zwingli and his adherents would judge this military service to be in essence contradictory to Christianity. It is almost impossible to determine whether this arrangement of military pay did indeed lessen the economic and demographic problems of the mountain districts, in particular, or whether it only created new difficulties.

The late medieval development of Switzerland finally led to a Confederate national consciousness. The concept "fatherland" (*patria*) underwent a change of meaning in which the term was no longer applied to a single region but rather to the Confederation as a whole.

Zwingli himself felt he was a Swiss who proclaimed Christ to the Swiss, and therefore declared emphatically to the bishop of Constance that one should not rank the Swiss with the Germans.[2] With these words — uttered with a certain amount of pride — Zwingli reflected the general attitude toward life that the Confederation regarded as "fatherland."

Therefore it is in no way a coincidence that a preoccupation with one's own history set in more passionately in Switzerland than elsewhere at the beginning of the sixteenth century. Swiss humanism concentrated on writing history, emphasized the coequality of the Confederation's past, but at the same time clung to its diversity, for this provided a greater degree of liberty. The past was contrasted with the alleged moral corruption and dissipation of contemporary society. As against the universal humanism of an Erasmus, who contemplated "being truly human," Swiss nationalistic and patriotic humanism aimed at a renewal of the fatherland. On the one hand, these efforts at reform are narrower, because they seem to be shaped by their Swiss background; but they are also more extensive, since they are aimed at society as a whole rather than at the individual. Zwingli's own reformatory goals remained committed to these humanist ideals.

William Tell, the most powerful symbol of Swiss national consciousness, was at this time associated ever more closely with the beginnings of the Confederation. Although Zwingli seldom mentioned him, he regarded this native of Uri as the founder of Confederation freedom who successfully defended himself against oppression and tyranny.[3] Confederation consciousness made use of the widespread William Tell legend after the second half of the fifteenth century; the integrative effect of a liberator and national hero furthered the concept of autonomy.

3. Zurich

a) Governmental Power and Political Institutions

In 1351, the Free City of Zurich joined the federation of Confederates, comprised at that time of the mountain districts of Schwyz, Uri,

Unterwalden, and Lucerne. This affiliation of a city-state, too, was governed by the menace posed by the Hapsburgs; the purpose was to insure Zurich's political independence.

A few years earlier, Zurich had experienced a profound political upheaval which resulted in the replacement of the aristocratic system of city government with a system based on the guild principle. Now the representatives of the craft guilds had become the equals of the knights and the nobles. This legal equality of artisans, and their organization into guilds under Mayor Rudolf Brun,[4] marks the beginning of Zurich as a guild city. In contrast to Bern, the aristocratic element became increasingly insignificant in Zurich, so that by the sixteenth century it was governed by the guilds, or rather, by their representatives. Zwingli's activities can be understood only against the background of the composition, authorization, and functioning of a Zurich government organized in this way.

The Large Council exercised the supreme legal power in the city-state. Its members had to belong to one of the thirteen guilds. Twelve guilds each had twelve representatives on this governing board. In addition, there were eighteen members of the Society of Constabulary.[5] Since this society encompassed the knights, merchants, property owners, and financiers, it was not a guild in the strict sense of the word. The 162 councilmen were not elected by the guilds; instead, each representative chose his own successor.

But the greatest political power was actually exercised by the Small Council. Its members did not come from the Large Council; rather, they went beyond the Large Council and once again represented all the guilds according to a complex formula. At the head of these twenty-five councilmen was a mayor. Two of these governing boards were appointed, and each governed for six months at a time. The quick turnover in the Small Council did not work out well in practice, so that eventually both governing boards were allowed to meet together. It became customary to designate this college of fifty councilmen the Small Council.

The Small Council was obliged to include the governing board of the 162 in the matter of far-reaching regulations. Together, this "Council of Two Hundred" (to be accurate, 212 members) made decisions about alliances, exceptional taxes, war and peace, buying and

selling of districts, new appointments to important positions, certifi-
cation of and instruction for ambassadors, and courts of appeal. This
combined governing body was called "mayors, councils, and citizens"
in Zurich, and could be activated only at the instigation of the Small
Council.

Since after the beginning of the sixteenth century the Large Council made a special point of supporting the interests of a broader urban
economy whereas the Small Council, in comparison, favored the
urban elite, tensions were created that would be aggravated with
regard to decisions on church affairs at the time of the Reformation.
This balanced system of power could not prevent the members of the
constabulary, as well as the members of the guilds of Meise and
Safran, from having a leadership role in practical politics, since this
is where the most powerful dealers and artisans could be found. The
social elite and the most economically powerful people in Zurich thus
determined the course of the city. This conclusion can be drawn on
the basis of the so-called ordinances of councilmen, which were
examined in detail by Walter Jacob and Hans Mork, disciples of
Leonard von Muralt.

This arrangement also provides the key to understanding the possibilities for political effectiveness available to Zwingli, for both Small
and Large Councils appointed "counselors" (*Verordnete*) to prepare
council decisions in all important political and ecclesiastical questions. Zwingli used a Greek expression to designate them as "people
who should give preliminary counsel."[6] In most cases, the council
governing board turned the recommendations that the counselors
usually submitted in writing into ordinances.

The composition of any given advisory commission, like that of the
foreign affairs delegations (for example, to the Diet) was not fixed
constitutionally, and therefore provided a picture of the actual distribution of power. Since the category of counselors and their membership in guilds is easily determined from the sources, continuity and
variations can be measured over a longer period of time. The same
councilmen were repeatedly appointed to deal with particular types
of problems, which lets us recognize specialization among the politicians. The members of these commissions usually belonged to the
Small Council, and the majority of the delegates were from the three

most powerful economic groups (Constabulary, Meise, Safran). With regard to foreign policy regulations, one-half of all delegates until 1516 were from the Society of Constabulary; their participation decreased after that, for reasons that are not yet clear. It is possible that this change is the reason for Zurich's foreign policy reorientation to favor the pope. A weakening of the influence of the men of the Constabulary can also be seen in other matters, such as in the city's financial administration. The craft guilds increased in importance in Zurich as well as in comparable cities. Immediately before Zwingli's appearance, the actual balance of power was already shifting, even though the constitutional structure was not.

The preliminary advisory committees had great influence, even though the counselors could never have assumed control either legally or in practice. "Mayors, Councils and Citizens held the reins of government."[7] Zwingli's direct political activity was limited to participation in these advisory commissions. He was an equal member of the governing board, or he wrote expert opinions for the commission, or else he presented his views orally to the commission. Thus the reformer was never able to bring about an immediate political decision in Zurich.

b) Economy

In Zwingli's time, the city of Zurich had a population of about 5,000 and was therefore at the same level as Bern and Freiburg, but far behind Basel and Geneva, each of which had about 10,000 inhabitants. Like the rest of Europe, the population in the Zurich territory increased quickly after about 1470, with the result that by 1530 the population had nearly doubled in the city-state—from about 28,000 to about 53,000. Along with other factors, this "population growth led to basic upheavals in the late medieval price and wage structure. An increasing scarcity of food and land was set against an increasing labor force."[8] Attempts were therefore made to cultivate land more intensively and to gain new land by clearing and purchase. Yet these measures could not prevent a rapid acceleration of property fragmentation, which led to greater indebtedness and impoverishment; the result was a subpeasant class of day laborers and landless agricultural workers. This rural proletariat's only alternative to service in foreign armies — which was not permitted — was to accept government welfare. In any case, economic privations were most sharply felt in rural areas.

After the collapse of the Zurich silk industry, which had bloomed in the fourteenth century and had supplied a supraregional market, Zurich's industrial importance was confined to its own territory by the beginning of the sixteenth century. Trade was of greater importance, since the city's location on the periphery of the Alps was a favorable transfer point for the exchange of goods between the Swiss interior and Upper Germany. The cattle-raising alpine regions were especially dependent on deliveries through Zurich, because they had to buy their indispensable salt from the Salzburg region and from Tyrol, and the necessary supplementary grain from the Upper Rhine and Danube regions. During the Old Zurich War, this city on the Limmat river had, by erecting a trade barrier, caused the embittered and ultimately successful counterattack of the mountain inhabitants. This occurrence would be repeated at the time of the Reformation.

Zurich's economy was thus based on regional cattle, grain, and salt trade on the one hand, and on agriculture on the other hand. There is evidence of a recession in both these areas immediately before the Reformation, the causes of which have not yet been fully explained. The peasants complained about restrictions in the trade of agricultural products, artisans witnessed a rise in the cost of living, and rich prebendaries discovered a decrease in their wealth. Many people blamed the mercenary service abroad and the pension arrangement for the deterioration of the economic situation. The pension arrangement was an extremely suitable symbol for the general distress and — depending on one's position — the emphasis was on its moral, political, economic, or national aspect.

c) Church

Despite adequate source material, researchers have neglected Zurich church life in the late Middle Ages. As long as Zurich's relationship to the Constance bishopric, or the composition of the Zurich clergy, or the spiritual and financial status of its religious institutions and monasteries, or the religious life of the city have not been examined more thoroughly, it is difficult to place Zwingli's conflicts at the start of his reformatory activity in proper context or to assess them properly. As a result, the question of the continuity or discontinuity of the Zurich government's decisions about the church can only be answered provisionally, even though any judgment about Zwingli's work is essentially dependent on it.

The district of Zurich canton, along with the greatest part of the northeastern Confederation, belonged to the diocese of Constance, which, together with its districts on the right bank of the Rhine in the Black Forest, Upper Swabia, and Allgau, led all German dioceses in size and number of souls. At the time of the Reformation, it encompassed about 1,800 parishes and 350 monasteries, with over 15,000 priests. After 1496, it was headed by Bishop Hugo von Hohenlandenberg (1460–1532), who was descended from a Zurich family. Although he was certainly concerned with providing proper leadership for his diocese, and was filled with a will to reform, all his efforts were doomed to fail because of his personal shortcomings as model, and because of inherent difficulties of a political and church-political nature. Von Hohenlandenberg himself broke the commandment of chastity, favored relatives in his appointments to positions in the episcopal administration, and amassed prebends with revenues in Friesach (in Corinthia), Chur, Basel, Constance, and Erfurt.

On the one hand, the Constance cathedral chapter restricted the bishop's powers in making appointments to important offices, and on the other hand he had to take the members of the Confederation into consideration, since the diocese had entered into a formal concordat with them in 1493 (the so-called Second Pastoral Letter). The members of the Confederation had pledged to protect the secular property of the spiritual prince of the Holy Roman Empire on the left bank of the Rhine (called "umbrella right") if the bishop, for his part, would guarantee and respect their ancient rights with regard to church affairs.

The consequence of this episcopal concession was that political authorities could protect the clergy against the clutches of their head shepherd — an important source of revenue for the Constance curia, as in other dioceses, was the financial exploitation of the clergy. One particular problem was the rule of celibacy, or rather, the punishment for the sin of concubinage. The episcopal court, when declaring absolution for the violation of the vow of chastity, always imposed a fine calculated to accord with the severity of the transgression. Indeed, there were priests who obtained absolution regularly, so that the concomitant fine attained the character of a tax on the priest living in concubinage. Nor can it be denied that these same priests very often executed their pastoral duties conscientiously and were particularly respected by the people precisely because of the durability of their marriage-like life style. In no way did concubinage need to burden their relationship to their parishioners; the father of Zwingli's successor, Heinrich Bullinger, lived for decades as priest and dean in Bremgarten, unmolested and respected, with his wife and children.

Nevertheless, church verdicts impinged deeply on the financial condition of the pastor, and in some cases that of his children. The proliferation of taxes and fines naturally did not further the pastor's sense of duty; rather, it resulted in much greater bitterness against the bishop and his officials, particularly on the part of the lower clergy. The situation within the clergy was marked by a strong contrast between the high, property-owning clergy and the simple priests living in relative poverty.

About two hundred clergymen lived in the city of Zurich, which was a lower percentage, in comparison to the population as a whole, than in Geneva or Mainz, but nevertheless represented between 15 and 20 percent of employable men. Economic pressures on these clerics at times of recession led to their gradual impoverishment and resulted in the creation of an actual spiritual proletariat. Since priests delinquent in their payments were banned from presiding at worship services, an episcopal verdict had direct consequences for the parish. Therefore the parish was very interested in protecting its priests against the bishop's might.

Oskar Vasella, the greatest expert on the pre-Reformation church situation in Switzerland, concluded that the "Second Pastoral Letter" could in no way be construed as hostility toward reform on the part of the Confederate States. Instead, these states were "determined to prevent the draining of all too significant sums of money from the Confederation to Constance, but particularly to also set limits to the unworthy system of punishing the guilty through fiscal exploitation, and thus to obviate the clergy's growing discontent."[9]

In a pastoral letter dated May 3, 1516 (on the eve of the Reformation), Bishop Hugo himself complained about the deteriorated condition of the clergy: concubinage, gambling, quarrelsomeness, worldly behavior, setting a bad example. Despite his threats of punishment, the head shepherd failed to achieve any success at all in reforming either the secular priests or the monks in the monasteries. Even a man of greater willpower than Hugo would have been overtaxed in administering such a huge diocese, with its territorial, jurisdictional, and political diversity. After 1518, he had the help of Dr. John Fabri as his vicar general. Fabri was one of the ablest and most honorable leaders of those seeking reform but not joining the Reformation. It did not help much. But for the sake of the burgeoning Reformation in Zurich it was rather significant that he was not in Constance during the particularly decisive months of 1522 and was therefore not available to oppose Zwingli. One irony of history: While Fabri was in Rome trying to achieve more resolute proceedings against Luther, a comparable movement was developing in his own diocese.

On the basis of his ancestry as well as his above-mentioned traditional ties to Switzerland, Hugo pursued friendly political relations with the Confederation, and even deliberated about joining their federation. But, as a result of the Swabian War, his interest gradually shifted in favor of his imperial Hapsburg connections; this shift was later reinforced by the reformatory events in Zurich. In any case, when judging the bishop's conduct toward the burgeoning Reformation movement in Zurich, one must keep in mind that at this time Zurich was considered more friendly to Austria than any other state in the Confederation. The same political alignment could have convinced the bishop to proceed with caution against Zurich and its church-critical movement.

But the city government's concrete church-political measures did much more to repress and erode the bishop's power than the pastoral letter or the Constance cathedral chapter. The confederate city-states were an impressive example of this tendency, noticeable throughout the late Middle Ages. In Zurich, the government's intention to limit spiritual power and ecclesiastical property had existed since the thirteenth century, but made itself felt in the second half of the fifteenth century: the Small Council prohibited spiritual institutions, as well as clerics, to acquire property, and imposed a requirement that permission be sought before making any donation of property to an ecclesiastical foundation, in order to control the expansion of their properties. The city doggedly expanded its jurisdiction by taking into its own court all conflicts involving donations to the church, which had been reserved to the ecclesiastical court in Constance for decision. Since these disagreements about the obligation to pay interest and about tithing comprised the majority of civil suits, the government could by these means take a large step in the direction of total control of jurisdiction in its territory.

Marriage laws and the resultant constant legal proceedings had an even greater impact on the life of the people. Long drawn-out proceedings and high court costs before the Constance curia were a burden on all parties. There were so many marital cases from Zurich before the episcopal court that it appointed a special commissioner to Zurich whose duty was to decide about initiating legal proceedings. Since the city had been successful, as early as 1502, in having its own choice, Heinrich Utinger, appointed to this position, it did not hesitate to give the commissioner instructions regarding the initiation or denial of suits. It was hoped that this was a way to settle petty lawsuits out of court. Since every trial was linked to revenues, this naturally ran counter to the bishop's wishes. During the course of the Reformation, the city established a domestic relations court independent of the bishop. The same Heinrich Utinger served as court clerk.

Besides these governmental encroachments, which can be explained as concern for the economic well-being of the country's people, some measures touched on the area of the bishop's direct spiritual supervision. Pre-Reformation Zurich had already had laws regulating morality: prohibition of dancing and gambling, regulations against swearing, and blue laws. In 1507, the Council petitioned the bishop to take action against an unworthy priest; indeed, in 1512, since petitions to Constance were apparently useless, it turned to the pope himself with the plea to eradicate the scandalous system of concubinage. The Council had gone further in 1492, when it appointed a commission to investigate the Augustinian prior's sermons, which had caused offense; in typical fashion, he was accused of having incited unrest.

The city attempted to assume control over the deportment of monasteries and religious establishments early on, especially since these played a leading role in church life as well as in church politics. After great effort, the Council succeeded in obtaining the right to fill the most highly endowed posts at the Great Minster and at the abbey of the Mary Minster. The Large Council, which characteristically had the right to do so, naturally favored members of Zurich families for these positions, and thus set up one more barrier to outside and alien elements. At the same time, the Council thus assured solidarity within the city, and helped balance spiritual and city interests. This strategy forced clergymen to become citizens and thus subject to the city's jurisdiction. Moreover, toward the end of the fifteenth century, the Council increased its financial control by appointing monastery curators who administered the monasteries according to the will of the authorities, acted as consultants, and assisted in decision making. In addition to exercising this economic guardianship, the authorities also intervened in the domestic affairs of the monasteries; for example, the Council was able to prevent the monastic seminary (*Predigerkloster*) from joining the conservative trend within the Dominican order.

Strangely enough, Zurich does not seem to have known about the pre-Reformation establishment of a "preaching post" (*Prädikatur*), which Bern, Basel, Bremgarten, Chur, Winterthur, and other places had. It was precisely the endowment of such posts that testified to urban citizens' will to reform.

Zwingli's success cannot be explained by these elements of pre-Reformation church politics alone; however, just how great the alignment was between these elements and the innovations of the 1520s is evident.

The following detailed notes should serve to elaborate on the remark made above that religious foundations and monasteries had been the carriers of Zurich's ecclesiastical life. Since the ninth century, there had existed on the left bank of the Limmat River a choir school for secular choristers; to this Great Minster Foundation (*Grossmünsterstift*) was attached the parish church of St. Felix and Regula, dedicated to Zurich's patron saints. On the opposite bank of the Limmat, a Benedictine abbey called the Mary Minster (*Frau-*

münster) was erected in the same century. Admission to the abbey was eventually reserved to members of the nobility; by the beginning of the Reformation, the Mary Minster had already sunk into insignificance, and only the abbess, Katherine von Zimmern, still lived in the abbey. Seven canons and three chaplains worked in the church attached to the abbey; since this church had no regular clergy, St. Peter's Church became the actual parish church, even though its legal history is obscure. Twelve priests were employed there. Both Dominicans and Franciscans had establishments in Zurich; the Augustinian Hermits occupied a monastery of their own. A total of about fifty monks lived in these three establishments. Finally, there were a large number of Dominican nuns in two cloisters, in Oetenbach and St. Verena; and more monastic establishments could be found in the vicinity of the city. In view of this richness of religious institutions and monasteries, it is no wonder that, as people's priest in the Great Minster, Zwingli grappled with the monastic system very early.

Nothing certain can be said about the origin and education of the Zurich clergy, the number of whom rose to about five hundred in the total territory of city and countryside. One can presume that there were not as many trained theologians among them as there would have been in a city having a university or episcopal seat. This lack of experts, especially when it came to finding solutions to complex problems involving canon law, allowed Zwingli to succeed so easily in obtaining his position as consultant to the Zurich government.

In attempting to summarize Zurich's political and ecclesiastical circumstances on the eve of the Reformation, one can perhaps hold on to the following: Zurich, as one of the thirteen Independent States, plays a leading role in the Confederation, but has meanwhile isolated itself by turning away from a foreign policy friendly to the French and instead leaning toward the papal party. The situation within the city-state is marked by stability of political institutions, but the class of political leaders expands to favor craft guild members. The economic situation demonstrates a transition from stagnation to recession, which will lead to the impoverishment and pauperization of many urban and rural social classes. The city government, on the way to achieving complete sovereignty, pursues the goal of regulating all aspects of life (*Lebensaüsserungen*) on its territory, and therefore attempts to restrict the exceptional status of clerics and ecclesiastical institutions. Not even the domestic affairs of the church are safe. In any case, questions of church and faith are politically highly explosive in Zurich — as are other urban circumstances as well.

4. Bibliography

Beck, Marcel. "Wilhelm Tell. Sage Oder Geschichte?" *Deutsches Archiv zur Erforschung des Mittelalters* 36 (1980): 1–24.

Hauswirth, René. "Wie verhandelte das Parlament des Alten Zürich? Versuch einer Rekonstruktion von Ratsdebatten aus der Bullinger-Zeit." *Zürcher Taschenbuch* (1973, Neue Folge, 93d Jahrgang): 30–49.

Jacob, Walter. *Politische Führungsschicht und Reformation. Untersuchungen zur Reformation in Zürich 1519–1528* Zürcher Beiträge zur Reformationsgeschichte 1. Zurich, 1970.

Kobelt, Eduard. *Die Bedeutung der Eidgenossenschaft für Huldrych Zwingli.* Mitteilungen der Antiquarischen Gesellschaft in Zürich. 45 H. 2, 134th Neujahrsblatt.

Lengwiler, Eduard. "Die vorreformatorischen Prädikaturen der deutschen Schweiz. Von ihrer Entstehung bis 1530." Ph. D. diss., Freiburg, Switzerland, 1955.

Maeder, Kurt. *Die Via Media in der Schweizerischen Reformation. Studien zum Problem der Kontinuität im Zeitalter der Glaubensspaltung.* Zürcher Beiträge zur Reformationsgeschichte 2. Zurich, 1970.

———. "Die Bedeutung der Landschaft für den Verlauf des reformatorischen Prozesses in Zürich (1522–1532)." In Bernd Moeller, ed., *Stadt und Kirche im 16. Jahrhundert,* 91–98. Schriften des Vereins für Reformationsgeschichte 190. Gütersloh, 1978.

Moeller, Bernd. "Kleriker als Bürger." In *Festschrift für Hermann Heimpel zum 70. Geburtstag am 19. September 1971,* 2:195–224. Göttingen, 1972.

Morf, Hans. *Zunftverfassung und Obrigkeit in Zürich von Waldmann bis Zwingli.* Mitteilungen der Antiquarischen Gesellschaft in Zürich 45. H. 1, 133d Neujahrsblatt. Zurich, 1969.

———. "Obrigkeit und Kirche in Zürich bis zu Beginn der Reformation." *Zwingliana* 13 (1970): 164–205.

Muralt, Leonhard von. *Zürich im Schweizerbund. Zum Gedenken an Zürichs Eintritt in den Bund der Eidgenossen vor 600 Jahren.* Zurich, 1951.

———. "Zum Problem der Theokratie bei Zwingli." In *Discordia Concors. Festgabe für Edgar Bonjour,* 2:367–90. Basel and Stuttgart, 1968.

Peyer, Hans Conrad. *Verfassungsgeschichte der alten Schweiz.* Zurich, 1978.

————. "Die wirtschaftliche Bedeutung der fremden Dienste für die Schweiz vom 15. bis zum 18. Jahrhundert." In *Könige, Stadt und Kapital. Aufsätze zur Wirtschafts- und Sozialgeschichte des Mittelalters,* 219–31, 309–10. Zurich, 1982.

Sigg, Otto. "Bevölkerungs-, agrar-, und sozialgeschichtlich Probleme des 16. Jahrhunderts am Beispiel der Zürcher Landschaft." *Schweizerische Zeitschrift für Geschichte* 24 (1974): 1–25.

Vasella, Oskar. "Über die Ursachen der Reformation in der Schweiz." *Zeitschrift für Schweizer Geschichte* 27 (1974): 401–24.

————. *Reform und Reformation in der Schweiz, Zur Würdigung der Anfänge der Glaubenskrise.* 2d ed. Katholisches Leben und Kämpfen im Zeitalter der Glaubensspaltung 16. Münster, 1965.

Vögeli, Alfred, ed. *Jörg Vögeli, Schriften zur Reformation in Konstanz 1519–1538 II/1* Schriften zur Kirchen- und Rechts-geschichte 40. Tubingen and Basel, 1973. A portrayal of the life and work of Bishop Hugo von Hohenlandenberg until 1518 is found on pp. 489–625.

II

CHILDHOOD
AND STUDENT YEARS

1. The Problem of a
Zwingli Biography

If one turns to the inherent problem in any presentation of Zwingli's life and work, one is struck by how little thought has been given to it. What applies to Zwingli research in general also applies here: Despite a plethora of literary evidence, methodological questions have seldom been addressed. Zwingli research as a whole does not have a very pronounced awareness of methodology. A few fundamental problems follow.

Zwingli's life clearly breaks down into two periods: (1) the pre-Zurich time of Zwingli's youth, his student years, and the following twelve years of pastoral activity in the mountain district of Glarus (1506–1516) and in the pilgrimage place of Maria Einsiedeln (1516–1518); and (2) his time in Zurich. Although Zwingli's move to Zurich was to another pastorate, his social and ecclesiastical environment was totally different from his previous parishes. Moreover, since his criticism of the church began soon afterward, his inner presuppositions regarding his effectiveness must also have changed.

Sources for the whole pre-Zurich period are extremely meager. A few facts concerning Zwingli's parents and siblings, as well as his childhood years, have been handed down, but they stand out so little that no connections — to say nothing of possible explanations — can be derived from them with regard to his later effectiveness. The superficial data of his education are known (schooling in Weesen, Bern, and

Basel; studies in Vienna and Basel); we also know the names of a few of his teachers. But we have no certain knowledge regarding his courses of study or his influential teachers; and scarcely any information regarding his fellow students. The whole process of Zwingli's education and formation remains veiled in obscurity. It is impossible to do more than give a general description of the intellectual climate existing in the places in which he lived, and to mention some possible or probable impressions he might have had. There are more documents pertaining to his time in Glarus and Einsiedeln, yet here too there are many gaps—in the account of his pastoral activities, for example—and once again only the background can be sketched.

The situation regarding his inner development is scarcely better. The few reports Zwingli wrote during this period do not permit any judgment to be made regarding his intellectual development. That is why one must rely on his own retrospective views and on conclusions arrived at indirectly on the basis of his later theological writings.

There are two problems as a consequence: tendentious distortions are to be expected in his explicit retrospective statements, since Zwingli was concerned to present the pre-Reformation period in a certain light. Every reformer judges his religious-theological past negatively. Therefore Zwingli's recollections on this subject must be interpreted even more cautiously than must in any case be done with any autobiographical remarks. Furthermore, any interpretation of Zwingli's writings dating from the Reformation period confronts the essential question of whether the presuppositions and basic structure of his thought had remained unchanged despite his shift to the Reformation. Can there even be any talk of continuity between pre-Reformation and Reformation periods? In any case, the use of later writings to illumine his pre-Reformation period is on extremely shaky ground, which cannot be made any more solid through methodology.

Any depiction of Zwingli's Zurich period after 1522 really confronts the opposite problem: the great diversity of Zwingli's activities, recorded in a wealth of written accounts, confronts the biographer with the almost insurmountable difficulty of not losing sight of the overall connections between these countless fields of activity. When dealing with his multilevel environment, Zwingli functioned as preacher, exegetical teacher, theological author, church leader, and political consultant.

Thus every Zwingli portrayal must steer around two reefs: on the one hand the diverse aspects of his work must be related to each other; and on the other hand, possible changes in his presuppositions must be taken into account. Not many works on Zwingli have succeeded in satisfying both of these requirements. Some biographies suffer by neglecting the theological aspect, and picture Zwingli as essentially a statesman and church politician. But theological treatises often neglect the concrete reasons for Zwingli's development, and proceed heedlessly to a systematic portrayal of "Zwingli's theology." To be sure, the reformer seems to have made it easy for his interpreters, since he published five summaries of his thoughts.[1] Moreover, these writings only represent the Zwingli of 1523, 1525, 1530, and 1531, and address very specific people. He went through at least some development with regard to a few specific issues. Therefore one will have to guard against any harmonizing at all of his statements without sufficient reason.

2. Family, Childhood, School Years (1484–1498)

Zwingli came from a peasant family living in the high Toggenburg valley, which was more important to through traffic in the late Middle Ages than it is today. His name stems from *Twing*, meaning a fenced-in farm property. He himself sometimes thought of "twin," which is why he called himself "Gemini" (*Geminius*) in Latin texts. Opponents linked his name to "constrain" (*Zwingen*), and accused the "enforcer" (*Zwingel*), as Luther was to call him, of dealing violently with Scripture.

His father, also named "Ulrich," played a leading role as so-called administrator (*Amtmann*) in the local administration of the rather well-to-do peasant community of Wildhaus and, like grandfather Henry, was probably a small trader. There are two clerics in the family in the parents' generation: Bartholomew, one of the father's brothers, was the incumbent of the deanery in Weesen on Wallen Lake, after having been pastor in Wildhaus; the mother's first marriage had been with a close relative of the abbot of the Toggenburg Benedictine monastery of St. John.

Not much is known about Zwingli's siblings. There were at least nine of them. Two younger brothers became clerics: Jacob became a

Benedictine, studied in Vienna, but died as early as 1517; Andreas probably belonged to the same order; he came to Glarus, where he died in 1520 as the result of the plague. Two sisters probably became nuns. The other brothers remained loyal to farming.

On January 1, 1484, Zwingli was born into a family that had been raised above the average due to its social position and its ties to the church. He left home at age five to obtain his primary schooling on the other side of the mountain, and lived with his uncle Bartholomew in Weesen. We know nothing else about the five years he spent in Weesen.

In 1494, ten-year-old Zwingli was sent to Basel to obtain his secondary education. He lived with Magistrate Gregory Bünzli, a native of Weesen who was to teach him Latin. After three years in Basel, he stayed for a short time in Bern with the famous humanist Henry Wölfflin.

According to the accounts of Heinrich Bullinger and Johannes Stumpf, Zwingli was removed from Bern by his father and his uncle because the Dominicans were urging him — because of his beautiful voice — to join their order. It is possible that he had already made formal connections with the Bern Dominican monastery, since he did not refute later opposition claims that he had been a monk in Bern.[2] But he was too young to have been a novitiate. There may be a grain of truth in the story of energetic intervention on the part of the adults, insofar as Zwingli left Bern prematurely, without having completed his Latin studies. At least it can be concluded with some certainty that Zwingli had already come into contact with the monastic life style in his early years. It is impossible to date his stay in Bern more accurately; it probably occurred between the end of 1496 or the beginning of 1497 and the summer of 1498.

3. University Studies in Vienna and Basel (1498–1506)

Zwingli was matriculated at the University of Vienna for the winter semester 1498 under the name "Udalricus Zwinglij de Glaris." This is the first date of his life secured by documentary evidence. Since his native village of Wildhaus was too insignificant, he followed the custom of the time and claimed a larger town in its vicinity as his place of origin; and for the almost fifteen-year-old boy this was Glarus. His choice of university is not surprising, since a large number of Swiss studied on the banks of the Danube at the beginning of the sixteenth century. However, his stay there is itself one of the most impenetrable periods of his life.

Conditions at Vienna University at that time have not been researched very well. One does not know about the teaching activity, nor is one informed about the apparently close ties between the university and the city's Higher Latin School curriculum. As his brother Jacob did later, Huldrych Zwingli could have had connections with the Viennese Schotten monastery; possibly he did not complete his Latin studies until he was in Vienna.

Since another — but contemporary — hand added the word *exclusus* (expelled) to the matriculation entry mentioned above, yet Zwingli is nevertheless enrolled again for the summer semester of 1500, there has been a lot of guessing for a long time about what the word *exclusus* could possibly mean. There are no valid sources to show Zwingli's attendance at another university between 1498 and 1500. Although various vague sixteenth-century allusions speak of early ties to Tübingen, Cologne, and above all Paris, where he could have studied, they must be considered improbable until better evidence is produced. The simplest explanation for the *exclusus* is that a later Zwingli opponent added it in order to clear the University of Vienna of its humiliation for having "formed" an enemy of the church; for the way the entry *exclusus* was made, without a date and without a reason, does not conform to what was customary.

A second matriculation need not presuppose expulsion or interruption of study, since enrolling more than once occurred frequently at the University of Vienna, especially during this time. Most probably, therefore, Zwingli studied uninterruptedly from 1498 to 1502 at the University of Vienna, and his life was not marked by any unusual events. We do not know whether the excellent humanist teachers in Vienna made any deep impression at all on the not yet eighteen-year-old. In any case, Zwingli never mentioned them, and his first biographer, his friend and comrade-in-arms Oswald Myconius, dealt with the whole Viennese period in one sentence.

An assessment of these three and one-half years of study on the basis of available sources will not go beyond J. V. Pollet's conclusion that Zwingli's horizon was expanded to encompass all of Europe during this time, and that his transfer to Basel University for the summer semester of 1502 was a reversion to provincial circumstances.[3]

In Basel, Zwingli ended his liberal arts studies in the beginning of 1506 by receiving the Master of Arts degree (*Magister*). That is why later official Zurich documents would refer to him as Master Huldrych Zwingli. He studied theology for another six months, until the summer.

On the whole, not much more is known about his time in Basel than about his time in Vienna. It is almost certain that he earned his keep by teaching Latin. Of his professors, it was probably Thomas Wyttenbach (1472–1526) who had lasting influence on him. This Tübingen Master of Liberal Arts, who was from Biel, represented the philosophical school of the *via antiqua* in Basel. He based his academic teaching on the works of Thomas Aquinas and of Peter Lombard, with the commentary by Duns Scotus. Thus he used the classic traditional scholastic textbooks, in contrast to the *via moderna* of someone like William of Ockham, the guiding spirit of young Luther.

In Basel, Zwingli could have had his first encounters with humanist aspirations which, in an environment of printers, were aimed at the publication of classical and patristic authors. This is where he met Konrad Pellikan and Leo Jud, who would later be his friends and colleagues.

The assertion often advanced in the most recent Zwingli research, that he was influenced by Ulrich Surgant (ca. 1450–1503), also a professor at the university and the author of a widely disseminated handbook for pastors, has by no means been established as fact. Surgant's suggestions regarding the form of reformatory worship services in Zurich could certainly have been communicated solely by literary means.

4. The Fruits of Education

Zwingli went through a customary late medieval education, which was primarily directed toward the thorough acquisition of Latin, acquaintance with fundamental philosophical concepts, adoption of the traditional Aristotelian world view, and the ability to present thoughts and insights in an orderly manner both orally and in writing. At the end of his studies, Zwingli moved in the sphere of the *via antiqua* within the philosophical and theological currents of his day — a conclusion that can be drawn on the basis of some of his later statements. Hence it could also follow that his two predecessors in the Zurich position of people's priest (*Leutpriestertum*) were also counted among the realists; there was probably a tradition to that effect at the Great Minster.

Moreover, as was pointed out by J. F. Gerhard Goeters in particular, it was probably Duns Scotus — within the full scope of the *via antiqua* — who had the greatest influence on Zwingli. More specific things can be said only when an evaluation is made of his marginal notes to Duns Scotus's commentary on the *Sentences*, which Zwingli studied thoroughly.

On the whole, Zwingli's early life and his student days up to 1506 reveal nothing that would lift him above his contemporaries. However, his primary education under well-known teachers, his studies for several years at two universities, and his Master of Arts degree place him in a small minority among university graduates.

5. Bibliography

Blanke, Fritz. "Zwinglis Theologiestudium." *Theologische Blätter* 15 (1936): 94–95.

Bonorand, Conradin. "Die Bedeutung der Universität Wien für Humanismus und Reformation, insbesondere der Ostschweiz." *Zwingliana* 12 (1965): 162–80.

Edelmann, Heinrich. "Die Ammänner Zwingli 'zum Wilden Hus.' " *Zwingliana* 11 (1960): 193–97.

Goeters, J. F. Gerhard. "Zwinglis Werdegang als Erasmianer." In *Reformation und Humanismus. Robert Stupperich zum 65. Geburtstag*, 255–71. Witten, 1969.

Schmidt-Clausing, Fritz. "Johann Ulrich Surgant, ein Wegweiser des jungen Zwingli." *Zwingliana* 11 (1961): 287–320.

III

PASTORATE IN GLARUS
AND EINSIEDELN
(1506–1518)

1. Pastorate in Glarus
(1506–1516)

Like many of his contemporaries, Zwingli went into church work
soon after his examination for the Master of Arts degree, without
having studied much theology. In the diocese of Constance, candi-
dates for ordination into the priesthood were required to take an
examination, which was meant to test knowledge of dogma, mastery
of Latin in translating and interpreting a text, familiarity with the
liturgy of the mass and the calendar of feasts, as well as ability in pastoral care. When, or even whether, Zwingli took this examination is
not certain; it is possible that, on the basis of his master's degree, he
was exempt. In any case, he was ordained in Constance in September
1506, after having preached for the first time in Rapperswil. In
accordance with the custom of the time, Zwingli celebrated his first
mass in his hometown on St. Michael's Day, September 29, 1506. It
can therefore be said that the budding priest had an untroubled relationship with his family in Wildhaus.

The process of obtaining the pastorate in Glarus brought Zwingli
into contact with the world of ecclesiastical office peddling. Since
Heinrich Göldli, a notorious Zurich prebend hunter, was legal owner
of the pastorate, Zwingli had to satisfy Göldli's claims by making a
financial arrangement; every year he paid ten gulden to this collector
of offices out of his personal income.

The Confederate State of Glarus bordered on the district of

Weesen, and its capital was only about a two-hours' journey away. Thus Zwingli had returned to his homeland. However, Glarus was located in the diocese of Constance, as opposed to Weesen and Wildhaus, which were part of the diocese of Chur. Because of its size and population, Glarus was one of the smallest Independent States of the Confederation. The capital, of the same name, had a population of about thirteen hundred, and Zwingli and his three or four assistant priests were responsible for their spiritual care.

Not much is known about his activities. The few existing reports leave no room to doubt the uninterrupted ecclesiasticism of the pastor of Glarus. More light is shed on the first political position Zwingli took, an unavoidable one for a priest in a community like Glarus: in the controversy over whether Glarus should align itself with the French, the Hapsburgs, or the pope — and therefore who would have the disposition of the mercenary troops — Zwingli placed himself decisively on the side of the Roman See, and loyally clung to that position. The pope honored his attitude by paying him a certainly not negligible annual pension of fifty gulden. For the sake of comparison: no one was considered poor in Zurich unless they possessed less than twenty-five gulden. Zwingli had become a pension recipient himself.

His first literary works, written at this time, reveal how little he had been forced to make any political commitments. He expressed himself candidly about the events of the day, and showed no recognizable trace of restraint regarding secular affairs, either on general Christian principles or on the basis of ecclesiastical-priestly motives.

The Poetic Fable About the Ox[1] clothed the most recent history of the Confederation in the form of a fable in which the political powers appear as animals. In the autumn of 1510, Zwingli wished to warn his compatriots against entering into the service of either France or the emperor in exchange for money and gifts. He declared that the Confederates should unhesitatingly and with ancient loyalty rush solely to the aid of the pope.

Two years later, when the Confederate States ended an Italian campaign with the triumphant capture of Pavia, Zwingli praised this culmination of Confederate soldiership in the *Report of the Military Conflicts Between the French and the Swiss (De Gestis inter Gallos et Helvetios relatio).*[2] It is not certain that Zwingli actually took part in the campaign against Pavia. In any case, he understood "this whole Confederation undertaking for the defense of the pope as a matter of national honor. . . . The Swiss are not only the liberators of the church, they are the instrument of punishment against the enemies of the bride of the crucified Christ, weapon of the Crucified Himself. This high morale stimulates preachers to praise the Confederates as the people of God who have inscribed God's cause on their flag."[3] As a reformer, Zwingli would later express similar sentiments but would replace "Confederation" with "Zurich."

The Glarus pastor saw great military achievements in the extension of the Confederation wars of liberation; as a result, he was convinced that war is a justified means of preserving political freedom, the highest good.

The date for the third work, entitled "The Labyrinth" (*Das Labyrinth*)[4] in imitation of the Theseus myth, is uncertain, but is probably between 1514 and 1516. It is possible that Zwingli did not write the work — which survives as a fragment — in one sitting. The subject matter is once again an artfully adorned literary account flowing into a general admonition, which permits the inference that it was written at an advanced stage of Zwingli's development. Three other Zwingli writings of his pre-Zurich period have been lost: *The Plague (Pestis),*[5] *A Summary of the Gospel (Summa evangelii),*[6] and *Dialogue (Dialogus).*[7]

The Italian theater of war is the actual background of the works that survived; furthermore, Zwingli did not just know it from hearsay. Even if it is not certain that he took part in the Pavian campaign, he undoubtedly did take part in the battle near Novarra in 1513; and, above all, he accompanied the Glarus troops of about five hundred men in the disastrous war of the summer of 1515. The evidence for this Italian trip is a sermon Zwingli preached in Monza on September 7, 1515, in which he urged the Confederate States to reach agreement.

That campaign only lasted a month, but it ended with the crushing defeat at Marignano, which affected Zwingli personally in several respects. Following this defeat, the mood in Glarus shifted in favor of the French party, and Zwingli, the papal partisan and propagandist, found himself in an untenable position. He was forced to retreat. At any rate, his personal experiences on this bloody battlefield accelerated his thoughts on pacifism and solidified his total rejection of mercenary service. Zwingli personified the truth of Erasmus's favorite saying in defense of pacifism, "War is pleasant (only) for the inexperienced" (*Dulce bellum inexpertis*). The Glarus pastor underlined this sentence in his personal copy of Erasmus's collection of proverbs.

2. Pastorate in Einsiedeln
(1516–1518)

Einsiedeln (Canton Schwyz) had been widely known since the early Middle Ages because of its Benedictine monastery, founded in the ninth century, and its shrine to Mary. Pilgrimages to it had been made since the thirteenth century. Maria Einsiedeln's popularity reached its peak in the fifteenth century as far as the number of visitors as well as distance traveled by the pilgrims was concerned. Pilgrims even came to the Swiss interior from as far away as the Baltic Sea. No wonder the Einsiedler humanist Albrecht von Bonstetten (ca. 1443–ca. 1504) wrote the history of its founding and had it printed in Ulm!

Zwingli's only decisive reasons for leaving Glarus were political ones, namely, opposition from the friends of France. His reasons for choosing Einsiedeln are not known. Perhaps longer-standing connections to influential people there played a role.

Zwingli assumed the post of people's priest at the Benedictine abbey in late 1516, with the responsibility of providing pastoral care to both the inhabitants of the valley and to the pilgrims. He was not obliged to participate in the life of the monastery. However, there really was not much of that to speak of anymore; the convent included only two members in this place of pilgrimage. The incumbent abbot was absent most of the time, and the other convent member, Diebold von Geroldseck, who was the same age as Zwingli, administered the extensive monastic property, and was obliged to concern himself more with financial affairs than with spiritual ones.

Zwingli worked in Einsiedeln only a little over two years, from November 26, 1516 to the end of December 1518. On the whole, this period is characterized by a total withdrawal from political interests in favor of ecclesiastical activity; above all, he devoted himself to personal studies, carried on in scholarly exchange with his circle of friends.

Details concerning the duties of a people's priest of that period are not known, and Zwingli did not report much about his activities. But the few available notes suggest that Zwingli devoted himself intensively to preaching. His sermons were moral admonitions rather than dealing with the prevalent themes of church piety like pilgrimages, indulgences, hellfire, veneration of saints, or penitential acts. However, since not a single sermon of his time in Einsiedeln has survived, this judgment remains uncertain. He still confined his criticism of ceremony to its excesses and exaggerations, and did not yet consider it to be conflicting in essence with Christianity. Otherwise he would scarcely have taken part in a pilgrimage to Aachen in 1517.

At this time, he received a call to serve as pastor and teacher in the provincial town of Winterthur in Zurich. Zwingli refused the call.[8] The reasons he gave—that the rulers of Glarus were opposed to his move, and that he was obliged to show consideration for his relatives—do not sound convincing. More likely he thought there were not enough opportunities for growth in Winterthur, for when he was called to the prestigious position of people's priest at the Zurich Great Minster, he no longer gave any sign of the reluctance that was considered a necessary part of politeness.

3. Inner Development

In addition to the ecclesiastical and political aspects already described, one of the most important elements of Zwingli's biography between 1506 and 1518 is his inner development and growth. This includes three decisive components: his reading of classical, patristic, and scholastic writings; his membership in the circle of Swiss humanists; and his literary and personal encounter with Erasmus.

A particular problem is posed by the condition of the sources, and this must first be dealt with in detail.

a) Sources

Zwingli donated his own library during his lifetime to the Great Minster Foundation in exchange for a sum of money paid to his children.[9] It was incorporated into the foundation's library and arrived at the central library of Zurich by way of the foundation's successor, the Canton Library; a portion of his collection has in fact survived there. Unfortunately, no catalogue has been transmitted, so that the extent of his collection has had to be reconstructed from Zwingli's writings, especially his letters, and from books that have been preserved.

Nevertheless, Jacob Werner and Walther Köhler managed to trace and identify about one hundred surviving books from Zwingli's collection. Zwingli's library contained a total of about three hundred to three hundred and fifty volumes, which is the upper limit of a contemporary scholar's library. Zwingli used books borrowed from friends, and other books available at the foundation library, besides his own. His bookshelves contained a large number of classical editions of the time, such as classical historians (Herodotus, Hesiod, Livy, Pliny, Thucydides), philosophers (Aristotle, Plato), rhetoricians (Demosthenes, for example), and writers (Aesop, Aristophanes, Euripides) as well as aids to their study such as basic grammars and dictionaries. Zwingli's growing preoccupation with the church fathers and their editions is well reflected in his collection: there are editions of Athanasius, Augustine, Basil the Great, Chrysostom, Cyprian, Gregory of Nazian, Irenaeus, and others.

In addition, his library contained a more modest scholastic section, the focus of which was the commentary to the *Sentences* by John Duns Scotus.[10] Zwingli possessed more individual works by Erasmus than by any other contemporary. Although an inventory of his library does not of itself make a statement regarding his world of ideas, it does point to his inclinations: it is a typical humanist's library, which, however, does not neglect the scholastic element.

A more direct key to Zwingli's development is the notes he made in the books he read. They were first evaluated by Johann Martin Usteri, who wrote his observations in two articles still valuable today. When reading his books, Zwingli corrected printing errors, emphasized particular passages by underlining or marginal lines, wrote cue words in the margins, indicated parallel passages contained in the Bible or in other literature (usually omitting source references), and sometimes added his own opinion of what he read, thus revealing his agreement or rejection.

Since Zwingli's handwriting changed over the years, as Usteri has proved, one can classify his marginal notes chronologically. For instance, Zwingli wrote the Latin lowercase "d" with a pulled-down bar in his pre-Zurich days, but not later. Thus there is no difficulty in attributing all of Zwingli's handwritten statements to either one or the other of the two stages of his life.

But these convenient presuppositions for making use of pre-Zurich marginal notes are misleading. First, since there are gaps in the existing library, one can imagine Zwingli using books of which we have no knowledge. Second, one cannot always identify Zwingli's handwriting with absolute certainty. Since his books passed into what amounts to public ownership, they were still used frequently by other people in the sixteenth century, for example, by his successor Heinrich Bullinger; and these others probably also wrote in their own comments. These necessarily short and scrawled remarks or underlinings do not always reveal characteristics that could be unequivocally attributed to Zwingli's handwriting. Finally, the entries are often very difficult to decipher; and the difficulty of interpretation is increased since, as has been said, Zwingli quoted other writings in the margin without identifying them.

Köhler's edition of marginalia (which is still incomplete)[11] does not reveal any of these difficulties; instead, it is burdened with serious editorial shortcomings, for example, with regard to deciphering the subject, attributing a remark to Zwingli, or marking a quotation. That is why the present edition can be used only with the utmost caution; a complete revision is urgently needed. But that so distinguished a scholar as Köhler can make this kind of mistake is a sign of the degree of difficulty involved.

A third clue to Zwingli's development before the year 1519 can be derived from his autobiographical statements, which W. H. Neuser was the first to investigate in an orderly, careful, and methodologically responsible manner. The reformer alluded to his own earlier development particularly between 1521 and 1524; these remarks apply almost exclusively to the time after 1516, and focus on his claim to have "preached the gospel" since 1516. But it is not clear what this "gospel" really was. Not until 1527 did Zwingli write about that — in a treatise directed against Luther, of course — ten years after the events he described, in the context of the Reformation changes already completed in Zurich and of his difference from Luther, which by then had become evident. Yet even this explanation was unclear and ambiguous, because Zwingli was less concerned with determining just what his early opinions had been than with proving that he had attained reformatory clarity even before Luther appeared on the scene.

As Wilhelm H. Neuser has shown, binding conclusions regarding Zwingli's pre-Zurich development can scarcely be drawn from these statements, since their formulation is to a large extent determined by the time they were written and by the people they addressed. However, they at least reveal that Zwingli perceived the year 1516 to have been a turning point. His silence regarding his past up to 1516 is by no means a coincidence; in the reformer's view, those were wasted years.

The last group of sources, his correspondence, presents the fewest problems, even though several letters are undated and their correct classification has not been absolutely settled. However, Zwingli researchers have no clear idea of what percentage of Zwingli's correspondence has actually been preserved. When one compares the extensive correspondence achieved by humanists, when measured by the sixteenth-century norm, with the few available items of Zwingli correspondence, one must conclude that most of his letters have been lost. What has come down to us is therefore incomplete to start with, and to this must be added the fact that the rigid humanist style of letter writing used by Zwingli and his friends does not permit us to catch many personal glimpses of him. Nevertheless, the letters to and by Zwingli are our most important source with regard to his development until 1522.

Finally, Zwingli's contemporaries made comments about his activities or about particular aspects of these activities. Heading the list is his early friend Oswald Myconius, whose biography is written in the style of a classical eulogy and does all it can to increase Zwingli's reputation. He emphasized Zwingli's early renunciation of scholasticism and his independent development. The portrayals by Bullinger in his history of the Reformation and by Johannes Stumpf in his "Chronicle" (*Chronika*) have a similar style of apologetics.

b) Further Development Through Reading of Classical,
Patristic, and Scholastic Works.

In contradistinction to many of his colleagues in the priesthood,
Zwingli continued his education by studying on his own in the par-
sonage. As an extension of his Basel theological studies, he worked
through Duns Scotus's commentary to the *Sentences* that he had
bought. He was not interested in any particular theological question,
but rather sought to deepen his own knowledge as a whole. In this
he stayed true to the *via antiqua*, as Köhler, Gottfried W. Locher, and
especially J. F. Gerhard Goeters have shown; he had already become
acquainted with it in Basel in the person of Thomas Wyttenbach. We
can, at this point, ignore the question of whether Duns Scotus can
still be considered part of the *via antiqua*, or whether he represented
a stage in disintegrating Thomism.

At any rate, Duns Scotus left his mark on the Glarus priest. Zwingli
would later refer to him affirmatively during the Eucharist controversy.[12] As a Scotist theologian, Zwingli adhered to the Aristotelian
world view; yet the consequences of his Aristotelianism have never
been investigated thoroughly. According to Köhler,[13] the following
Aristotelian elements can be discerned in Zwingli: an interest in the
natural sciences, especially biology and geology; an image of
humankind that considered the heart the life-center; a radical distinction made between body and spirit—the body dies, the spirit is
immortal; sense organs focus on the sensory and recognize only sensory things; and the idea that something worldly cannot produce
spiritual results.

This fundamental presupposition in Zwingli's understanding of
the world was to determine his doctrine of the Eucharist: What distinguishes a human being from animals and plants is cognitive ability. Zwingli's concept of God was in line with Aristotelian and
Thomistic philosophy, because Zwingli stressed the supreme and
absolute Being of God. This resulted in a belief in providence and in
predetermination. Indeed, it even determined his christological doctrine, which found its starting point not in the appearance of Jesus,
but in reconciliation of the wrathful God through Jesus' death on the
cross.

Zwingli research is as yet unable to establish the influence of scholastic theology more accurately, not to mention classifying it in stages. Goeters's summary conclusion will have to suffice: "Thus Zwingli must be considered, without essential reservations, a scholastic theologian of the Scotist school, with a common Catholic understanding of piety and priesthood, until the year 1513."[14]

A second element, which has already been hinted at, must be added to these determinative factors in Zwingli's intellectual world: Zwingli shared humanist aspirations; after the 1510 *Poetic Fable About the Ox*, these aspirations became tangible. On the whole, it remains unclear how the scholastic and the humanist elements are interrelated. In any case, the Glarus priest clearly demonstrated how little one can regard "humanism" and "scholasticism" as mutually exclusive opposites.

Zwingli corresponded with humanist friends: with St. Gallen's Joachim Vadian in Vienna; and with Henry Loriti, who came from the province of Glarus (thus the nickname Glarean), in Cologne. The few surviving letters are concerned primarily with new publications, tips on how to study, news of political events, sending books, and worries about mutual protégés. Religious themes play just as small a role, in this correspondence, as the patriotic element that is the principal element in Zwingli's works.

On the whole, it becomes evident that, in addition to pursuing his scholastic studies, Zwingli was proceeding with his reading of classical authors and was beginning to direct his attention to the church fathers. Unfortunately, the extent of this reading cannot be determined. It was probably not the religious content of the patristic literature that attracted him; he focused on the literary and formal qualities of the early Christian authors, although it is unlikely that he found them engrossing. At least it can be stated as a guess that this reading matter could have led Zwingli to one of his principal subjects after 1516: the problem of authority with regard to the life of the church as well as to the conduct of the individual. The question was, How was it really, in the beginning? The key to Zwingli's energetic tackling of Holy Scripture, which became evident after 1513, might be his search for authority. He began to learn Greek at this time in order to be able to read the New Testament in the original version.[15]

c) *Turn to Erasmus*

Zwingli, hungry for education, studied scholastic works, read church fathers, and learned Greek on the side. These three components produced the inner conditions for Zwingli's attraction to Erasmus. His meeting with the prince of humanism was facilitated by Glarean's move to Basel in 1514, and by Erasmus's stay in that city from August 1514 until May 1516. Glarean was supporting Erasmus and propagating his ideals. Thus Zwingli gained access to the celebrated scholar.

After 1515, the Glarus pastor read Erasmian writings intensively: the *Handbook of a Christian Fighter*, the anthology of proverbs, and the works on biblical exegesis are some examples. He wrote affirmative comments in these books. His meeting with Erasmus in person, which probably occurred in the spring of 1516, overwhelmed Zwingli.

Following that meeting, Zwingli expressed his deep admiration and devotion in a letter to Erasmus,[16] which is the only Zwingli letter that vain humanist preserved. Aside from ritualistic flattery, Zwingli honored the theological achievement of Erasmus: no one else deserved so much praise for his work on the New Testament; thanks to Erasmus, Zwingli had found another, new, liberating approach to Holy Scripture; for this he would be grateful all his life.

This is also the way he expressed it in his autobiographical retrospective notes. Erasmus had taught him to ignore the simple grammatical structure of the biblical reports and to look instead for the real meaning behind these reports, for the deepest thoughts travel in simple dress; the Bible's center is the proclamation of Christ, which Zwingli understood as an admonition to control one's passions and as an appeal to the spiritual powers in a human being. Through Erasmus, Zwingli's world view had been increasingly determined by an ever sharper distinction between the divine and the creaturely; it was important to him to prevent their blending.

This ethically determined Christianity resulted in visible consequences for Zwingli's private life as well as his public one. Zwingli resolved that, in his private life, he would satisfy the high moral requirements of the Erasmian ideal life, and in particular obey the requirement of priestly celibacy. Zwingli's turn to a relative pacifism, expressed in the *Labyrinth*, can be traced to the influence of Erasmus. Finally, Zwingli's shift of emphasis giving priority to preaching — which can be seen in Einsiedeln — accorded with the reformed Christianity of Erasmus. In the spirit of his master, Zwingli demanded and furthered a simple Christianity of deeds — as against the complicated daily life of a Christian piety overburdened by ecclesiastical regulations and commandments — along with education and enlightenment, which was intended to bring general improvement to human beings. That is how Christianity would be reborn. Zwingli wanted "an improvement of morals. It is not a matter of guilt before God; rather, it is a matter of temporal ethics guaranteed through the best philosophy."[17]

In his intensive exegetical and patristic studies in Einsiedeln, which led him to copy the Greek text of the Pauline epistles in his own handwriting, Zwingli did not yet see a contradiction to the prevailing teaching of the church. On the other hand, one can detect no reserve of any kind to the humanist prince on the part of Zwingli in his pre-Zurich days, so that he could be considered an unreserved Erasmian and outstanding adherent of biblical humanism when he arrived in Zurich on January 1, 1519.

Zwingli would never repudiate the following aspects of Erasmian theology: reality is continuously separated into the creaturely and the divine, and it is important to be very careful not to mix the two; it is the moral duty of a human being to remove himself or herself increasingly from the worldly, in order to come closer to the spiritual; the Bible teaches about divine things and derives its authority from this; there are gradations within Scripture, and the words of Jesus are the highest; the Bible and biblical statements have a pedagogical character.

4. Bibliography

Egli, Emil. "Der Zug der Glarner nach Monza und Marignano." *Zwingliana* 2 (1912): 484–86.

Goeters, J. F. Gerhard. "Zwinglis Werdegang als Erasmianer." In *Reformation und Humanismus, Robert Strupperich zum 65. Geburtstag*, 255–71. Witten, 1969.

Kesselring, H. "Zur Erklärung und Zeitbestimmung der Gedichte Zwinglis vom Ochsen und vom Labyrinth." *Zwingliana* 1 (1902): 294–312.

Köhler, Walther. *Huldrych Zwinglis Bibliothek*. Zurich, 1921. "Neujahrsblatt auf das Jahr 1921. Zum Besten des Waisenhauses in Zürich," 84th Stück.

Locher, Gottfried W. "Zwingli und Erasmus." *Zwingliana* 13 (1969): 37–61.

Meylan, Henri. *Zwingli et Érasme, de l'Humanisme à la Réformation*. In Henri Meylan, *D'Érasme à Théodore de Bèze. Problèmes de l'Église et de l'École chez les Réformés*, 149. Travaux d'Humanisme et Renaissance. Geneva, 1976.

Näf, Werner. "Schweizerischer Humanismus. Zu Glareans 'Helvetiae Descriptio.' " *Schweizer Beiträge zur Allgemeinen Geschichte* 5 (1947): 186–98.

Neuser, Wilhelm H. *Die reformatorische Wende bei Zwingli*. Neukirchen, 1977.

Rogge, Joachim. *Zwingli und Erasmus. Die Friedensgedanken des jungen Zwingli*. Aufsätze und Vorträge zur Theologie und Religionswissenschaft 26. Berlin, 1962.

———. "Die Initia Zwinglis und Luthers. Eine Einführung in die Probleme." *Luther-Jahrbuch* 30 (1963): 107–33.

Stayer, James M. "Zwingli before Zurich. Humanist Reformer and Papal Partisan." *Archiv für Reformationsgeschichte* 72 (1981): 55–68.

Usteri, Johann Martin. *Zwingli und Erasmus. Eine reformationsgeschichtliche Studie*. Zurich, 1885.

———. "Initia Zwinglii. Beiträge zur Geschichte der Studien und der Geistesentwicklung Zwinglis in der Zeit vor Beginn der reformatorischen Tätigkeit (Nach bisher zum Teil unbekannten Quellen)." *Theologische Studien und Kritiken* 58 (1885): 607–72; 59 (1886): 95–159.

Vasella, Oskar. "Die Wahl Zwinglis als Leutpriester von Glarus." *Zeitschrift für Schweizerische Kirchengeschichte* 51 (1957): 27–35.

Werner, Jacob. "Zwingli Bibliothek." *Neue Zürcher Zeitung* (February 24, 1921): nos. 287, 293.

Wernle, Paul. "Das Verhältnis der schweizerischen zur deutschen Reformation." *Basler Zeitschrift für Geschichte und Altertumskunde* 17 (1918): 227–315.

IV
AWAKENING IN ZURICH
(1519–1522)

1. The Call

The position of people's priest became vacant in the Great Minster in Zurich late in 1518. The previous incumbent, Erhart Battman, had been promoted to the rank of canon. The twenty-four canons who administered the foundation exerted quite a bit of influence on the public life of Zurich. The foundation had large financial means at its disposal because of its extensive properties. Its support of several pastorates in the immediate vicinity of the city guaranteed it the opportunity to advance people of its own choice. The people's priest and his three assistants were obligated to care for their church colleagues at the Great Minster. That is why this office constituted the seam between the foundation and the city parish, and why any choice of pastor had to take these circumstances into account.

By choosing Huldrych Zwingli, the canons brought in a man whose political views agreed with Zurich's hostility to France. After the crushing military defeats the Confederate States had suffered in 1515, relations with France had lost importance, and the Confederates moved to support the politics of Hapsburg and the pope instead. This shift had occurred with the essential participation of Zurich; as a matter of fact, Zurich determined Switzerland's foreign relations between 1517 and 1520. Moreover, Zurich's prestige-conscious politicians were probably pleased to see a man assuming the important post at the Great Minster who was respected and honored by everyone.

But the foundation's decisive reason for calling Zwingli was his theological ability and, in particular, his membership in the Swiss circle of humanists and in the Erasmian reform movement. At the foundation itself, the schoolmaster Oswald Myconius, as well as Canons Heinrich Utinger, Dr. Heinrich Engelhart, Master Erasmus Schmid, and Erhart Battmann were at least sympathetic to the humanist efforts in the areas of education and renewal. Even before Zwingli's arrival, the Great Minster could be considered a reservoir of excellently trained scholars who recognized the defects of the contemporary church, above all among the clergy, and who were driven by a desire for change. Reform of life at the foundation had already begun. Zwingli was elected because he was expected to protect the interests of the foundation vis-à-vis the city and, at the same time, to support its desires for reform. A great deal was expected from his preaching in particular; this was to be the focal point of his duties, as it had been in Einsiedeln.

Shortly before the time came, rumors surfaced in Zurich about moral derelictions Zwingli had committed in his previous parish. In an unreservedly candid letter to Heinrich Utinger, dated December 5, 1518,[1] Pastor Zwingli confessed to having enjoyed forbidden intimacies with women. His excuses were his youth, the secrecy of the actions, and his repentance for his derelictions, particularly since he had repeatedly vowed never again to touch a woman. The letter provides a good insight into Zwingli's Christianity, which was determined by his intention to improve life. His honesty made a good impression, for, less than a week later, the canons elected him people's priest. He arrrived in Zurich toward the end of the month, and assumed office on January 1, 1519, his thirty-fifth birthday.

2. The Preaching Task

Nothing is known about Zwingli's early preaching. We know neither on what occasions he had to preach nor how often he did so. Not a single one of his sermons before 1522 — either the topic or the text — is available. However, it is possible that some of these sermons were incorporated into later compositions or publications. The few indirect reports about them allow only for a few preliminary conclusions.

Even before he assumed office, Zwingli had had to explain orally to the foundation his concept of the preaching function. According to his explanation, Zwingli's intention was to proclaim "the story of the Savior Christ" on the basis of the Gospel of Matthew. On the first of January, 1519, he did in fact begin to exegete the first Gospel from the very beginning (so-called serial reading [*lectio continua*]). Thus Zwingli violated the prevalent practice of basing a sermon on the Gospel lesson of the particular Sunday. His motives for doing so are not quite clear. No doubt Zwingli recalled the most famous preacher of early Christianity, John Chrysostom, whose serial exegesis of Matthew had been preserved; Zwingli had a copy of it in his library, as well as a copy of the church father Augustine's sermons on John.[2] Moreover, Zwingli was acquainted with the practice of "serial reading" in the monastic breviary. But, above all, Zwingli was not so much concerned about a serial interpretation of a biblical book as such as about the depiction of the life and work of Jesus.

Zwingli logically went on to an interpretation of Acts after the Gospel of Matthew, followed by the Epistles to Timothy. This was the way he could unfold the basic story of Christianity from Jesus' day to that of Paul's successors.

When using this method, Zwingli was guided by pedagogical interests. He taught about the Savior and used his own words to let the Zurich church imagine the model of the early congregation with its proclamation of the gospel and its moral purity. This reveals that the focal point of Zwingli's sermons was the exhortation and will to achieve moral and ecclesiastical improvement in exactly the way it was represented by Erasmian reformed Christianity.

3. The Problem of Zwingli's "Reformatory About-Face"

Possibly still in 1519, but certainly after 1520, the Erasmian basis of Zwingli's thought was shaken and gradually replaced by a new conception which is neither Erasmian nor Lutheran, but which instead represented Zwingli's own theological model. There is no agreement in Zwingli research about either the exact process of this decisive development or its result. In essence, two different explanations had been attempted.

The older view[3] starts with the conception that Zwingli, formed by Erasmus, was a passionate adherent of the humanist movement until he came into contact with Luther's writings after 1519. According to this view, the Wittenberg reformer transmitted to Zwingli the correct understanding of the Pauline epistles and thus opened the Reformation doctrine of grace *(sola gratia)* to him, which made Zwingli back away from Erasmus. Without having gone through Luther's kind of *Anfechtungen* and doubts, Zwingli freed himself from the medieval church's world of ideas and surpassed Luther in his practical innovations. This leads Walther Köhler to the conclusion that Lutheranism and Erasmianism were the basic elements of Zwingli's theology, and that the connection between them was what constituted the originality of the reformer; that Zwingli stood at the intersection of humanism and Reformation, represented by the names Erasmus and Luther; and that, if especially the Zurich and Swiss authors denied Zwingli's "Lutheranism," this was merely a repetition of Zwingli's own tactical declarations that he had discovered the gospel independently of Luther.

In contrast to the claim that Luther played a decisive role in Zwingli's "reformatory about-face," Arthur Rich, in his pioneering investigation, could establish that Zwingli had not dealt with Luther's central theological convictions until well into 1520, and that he had paid no attention to any of the three great "Reformation" writings of 1520. According to Rich, Zwingli's reason for reading Luther was rather to find support for his own opinions regarding issues of church organization and church politics (i.e., celibacy, indulgences, tithing, papal power). Zwingli read Luther's writings as products of the humanist reform movement, from which, as Cornelius Augustijn has demonstrated, they cannot in fact be separated. The reformer impressed Zwingli above all as a polemicist against the secularized papal church — which, in the eyes of the man from Zurich, did not raise him above the limits of the humanist efforts at reform — and therefore Luther's theology played only a peripheral role in Zwingli's development.

Gottfried W. Locher modified Rich's view by asserting that Zwingli had never been an unreserved Erasmus follower, and had instead represented a scriptural principle that diverged from Erasmus as early as 1515-1516; this had opened the way to the Reformation insight which, however, could not be clearly ascertained until 1522. It must, however, be said in this regard that the only evidence to substantiate Zwingli's divergence from Erasmus as early as 1516 is confined to later statements by the reformer himself. Locher's thesis is not very tenable, in view of the other direct reports testifying to Zwingli's agreement with humanist reformed Christianity.

On the whole, it will be impossible to bypass Rich and return to the older viewpoint. There is no doubt that in 1519-1520 Luther had no decisive influence on Zwingli's development. If one wishes to describe positively how Zwingli proceeded from Erasmian Christianity to Reformation theology, the following three points must be considered:

There is no agreement on either what Erasmian Christianity is precisely, nor on how to define "Reformation." Therefore both starting point and end point of Zwingli's development are unclear. The "Erasmian" issue, at least, is to combine in one concept the particular reformatory positions represented by the Swiss circle of humanists around 1519. The term "biblical humanism"[4] could also be used. In view of the diversity of theological positions among sixteenth-century Protestants, the concept "Reformation" cannot be precisely defined historically. Although earlier—and still today, in confessional Lutheran research—it was commonly equated with the theology of the Wittenberg reformer, the precise meaning of the term is increasingly obscured in the literature. If the term is used anyway, it is to point out that what happened was disengagement from the traditional church and its doctrine. With regard to content, various ways of dealing with this newly won viewpoint can be imagined. Luther's theology was probably the most significant force, but it was in no way the only effective one.

Sources for this chapter of Zwingli's life are still extremely sparse. It is essentially the same kind of testimony as that from the Glarus and Einsiedler days: later autobiographical statements, casual remarks, letters, observations of contemporaries. Just how incomplete the surviving material is can perhaps be seen from the fact that only ten letters in Zwingli's handwriting have survived from the period between August 1520 and the end of 1521. No other direct statements by Zwingli from this important one-and-a-half-year period of his life exist.

The banal fact that Zwingli's new insight grew out of his lively relationship with his congregation and community is often over-looked. Zwingli's sermons were based on careful exegesis and thor-ough study of Christian tradition, and were preached by coming to grips with the prevailing circumstances in Zurich against the back-ground of the events around Luther. Thus Zwingli's development was determined by the (changing) circumstances in Zurich, the news about the exciting events concerning Luther (for example, at the Diet of Worms), and his own reading of the Bible, the church fathers, and contemporary literature. All these factors contributed to a greater or lesser degree to the formation of Zwingli's own theological stance. In this connection, one must take into account Locher's point that this was a matter of a slow process lasting several years.

At this point, we forgo making the hypothetical attempt to describe this development, and merely mention a few relatively well-established facts.

Soon after taking office in Zurich, some pessimistic notes crept into Zwingli's remarks about himself and his duties. His optimism was crumbling. This change was biographically foreshadowed by his severe bout with the plague in the second half of 1519; the people's priest had been hit hard existentially and had experienced the fragil-ity of his own life. Nevertheless, these experiences, which can cer-tainly be compared to Luther's *Anfechtungen*, did not lead to his theological about-face. His *Song of the Plague*,[5] composed during this period, is still in perfect agreement with traditional thinking.

Around the middle of 1520, Zwingli found himself in a dangerous situation, for the scholarly struggle for the renewal of Christianity had been transformed into a fight to the death, as the events around Luther were demonstrating. Zwingli himself encountered opposition in Zurich. The people's priest felt strongly attracted to the church father Augustine at this time. Years later, Zwingli would confess "to having learned about the power and meaning of the gospel from the writings of John and the treatises of Augustine."[6] Perhaps Augustine provides the key to understanding Zwingli's development at this time. There are other known examples from the time of the Reformation of Augustine aiding disengagement from humanist ideals.

However, with this discovery of Zwingli's "Augustinianism" (which can certainly be so expressed), one has not yet gone past his initial steps, so that the significance and dimensions of the discovery are still unclear. In any case, it appears that by 1522 Zwingli had resolved the authority problem that had so preoccupied him. After 1522, he dealt with the scriptural principle in a way that rejected the presuppositions of the humanist reform program, which strove for a renewal of the church while preserving the traditional authorities (Scripture, dogma, councils, papal authority). Zwingli replaced these with the reformatory conviction that Scripture is the sole basis of teaching and life. After 1522, Zwingli no longer acknowledged the teaching authority of pope and councils who guard the correct use of the Bible. Scripture is open to everyone.

4. Critical Preaching

Only very slowly did Zwingli's changing theological stance influence the content of his sermons. These different stages could not be recognized in detail before 1522; we are, as we have said, dependent on statements of friends and opponents. According to them, the people's priest dealt from the pulpit with the usual topics of humanist criticism of the church. However, as his observant opponent, Canon Konrad Hofmann, noticed in retrospect in 1522, more far-reaching doubts of ecclesiastical tradition were already being mixed in with his usual scolding. Zwingli ranted against general moral corruption, and named individual erring Zurich citizens by name. Bad preachers of the gospel, as well as "speculative" scholastic theologians and ecclesiastical lawyers, were denounced. He turned against one group of people in particular: monks. He accused them of indolence and high living. He said that in the confessional in Einsiedeln he had heard plenty of examples of their immoral life style. In view of the significance of the monasteries to Zurich's ecclesiastical life, such a penitential sermon must have aroused more than the usual attention.

But more important than this reproof directed to a particular group of people was his criticism of ecclesiastical piety and legal practice. In 1519, Zwingli specifically rejected the veneration of saints, although he (still) allowed their invocation.[7] In any case, he said, there were too many feast days for saints; it would also be necessary to distinguish between the true and the fictional accounts of saints, and to eradicate all mendacious legends. The people's priest cast doubts on hellfire, and asserted that unbaptized children were not damned; he questioned whether excommunication was of any use whatever; he clearly ranked the sermon above the celebration of the mass; and he lashed out against the drawn-out proceedings of the Corpus Christi festival.

The greatest explosive power, both theologically and socially, was contained in Zwingli's attack on tithing. Payments of interest and tithes were among the pillars of the economic system. Expressed in somewhat oversimplified terms, "interest" was understood to be either the obligatory payment for a cash loan or the assessed taxes on real estate regardless of the amount of revenue. Tax collectors could be individuals as well as juridical persons, for instance, clerical institutions. A "tithe" was originally a payment dependent on revenues, or a payment in kind (theoretically, 10 percent of profit) to the ecclesiastical authority that maintained the respective parish. Most of the time this was identical to the calling authority, the *Kollator*. Regular payments by the peasants constituted a principal source of income for ecclesiastical institutions like abbeys and monasteries; this financial arrangement was justified by explaining the spiritual duties of these institutions. That is why the tithe was considered not only a bearable bargain between peasants and ecclesiastical agencies, but also an arrangement by divine right which therefore, as a matter of principle, could not be altered. Since the practice of ecclesiastical authorities transferring their rights to tithes to secular institutions or individual persons had become commonplace, the spiritual character of tithing disappeared. No distinction between tithes and interest could be recognized any longer.

As other critics had also done, Zwingli attacked the claim that the tithe was a divine institution. He asserted that its earlier meaning of "contribution to the church" must be regained. He allowed the collection of interest as a practice of economic life to stand if, for example, a loan had been made. The particular point of his criticism of the tithing system lay in the fact that one of the contractually set duties of the people's priest was "to strive, from the pulpit and in confessional, and to make sure that the people subject to the foundation honestly pay their tithes and all other contributions."[8] Even if Zwingli did not directly call for refusal to pay the tithe, he did contradict the immediate economic interests of the foundation, and this was bound to lead to conflict with his superiors.

Public reactions to these critical sermons did not materialize until the spring of 1522. Meanwhile, opposition was growing, within the governing body of twenty-four canons, to his sharp personal attacks from the pulpit as well as to the far-reaching theological implications of his statements regarding the authority of Scripture. These opponents could refer to a letter of complaint from the elderly, highly educated, personally irreproachable Canon Hofmann (1454–1525), who had himself held the office of people's priest for several years at the beginning of the century, and who had been remarkable for his penitential sermons.

Zwingli's opponents remained a minority. In fact, when a vacancy occurred among the canons, Zwingli was called to fill the position on April 29, 1521. He was also delegated, however, to continue his duties as people's priest; this unusual combination was a departure from previous rules of the foundation, because now Zwingli combined in his own person both executive officer and supervisor.

In any case, this innovation unequivocally demonstrates the increased respect for Zwingli among his new colleagues at the Great Minster. He found the greatest support for his reformatory ideas among this group of canons. Later adherents and companions emerged from this circle: Erasmus Schmid (connected with Zwingli since 1518, died in 1546); Dr. Henry Engelhart (simultaneously people's priest and canon at the Mary Minster, died in 1551); Henry Utinger (intimately connected to Zwingli, godfather to his first child).[9] Added to these was Chaplain Caspar Grossmann (in Berne after 1528, died in 1545) and George Binder, Myconius's successor as school principal (died in 1545).

It is possible that the Zurich authorities had already reacted favorably to Zwingli's preaching as early as the fall of 1520. Heinrich Bullinger's *Reformation History* mentions a decree requiring preachers to base their proclamation on Holy Scripture as their criterion. However, no other source substantiates this government ordinance; that is why both date and content are uncertain.

Another political measure by the Zurich Council can scarcely be attributed to Zwingli's activity. In the spring of 1521, when the contract between the Confederation and the king of France with regard to military recruitment came up for renewal, Zurich opposed it and refused to sign the new contract. Yet it was obliged to grant the opportunity to recruit to the pope during the summer of that same year. Nevertheless, public opinion in Zurich turned more and more against the pension system, so that a general prohibition was introduced in January 1522 which, however, could not be enforced totally. These decisions on the part of the authorities surely did agree with Zwingli's convictions, although — contrary to past assumptions — he had very little direct influence on their realization.

5. The Beginning of
Public Controversy

a) Fasting Practices

Public controversy regarding Zwingli's preaching was ignited by the question of whether and to what degree church regulations — in the concrete case of Lenten rules of fasting — must be obeyed. The incentive was the ostentatious eating of sausages on the early eve of the first Fasting Sunday[10] in the house of the printer Christoph Froschauer. Zwingli himself confessed that the approximately one dozen participants consciously transgressed the fasting rule in order to proclaim Christian liberty.[11] Two smoked sausages were cut into small pieces and distributed to those present.

Is it mere coincidence that time of day, number of participants, and method of distribution are reminiscent of the New Testament last supper? Among those present were Zwingli himself and two other clerics, but Zwingli was the only one who did not eat. One of the clerics was Leo Jud, Zwingli's successor in Einsiedeln, who would later stand out, as pastor of St. Peter's in Zurich, for his radical ideas, which surpassed those of Zwingli. Among the lay people mentioned by name were several men who have become familiar in other documents because of their provocative acts. Some of them later turned away from Zwingli and joined the Anabaptists because they thought he did not go far enough.

Zwingli presumably held back because, on the one hand, he

expected nothing to result from an ostentatiously provocative act—
this kind of action contradicts the customary image of his tactics—
and, on the other hand, he wanted to preserve the appearance of
impartiality, since he suspected that greater controversy would
follow. The events in the Froschauer house became known very
quickly; other violations of fasting followed. The Council was forced
to intervene and started judicial investigations. The mood in Zurich
was one of excitement.

Two weeks after the sausage meal in Froschauer's house, Zwingli
expressed his opinion regarding the principle of fasting, which
proves, by the way, that he could, for good reason, interrupt his
"serial reading" (lectio continua). The sermon was published in
expanded form on April 16, 1522, under the title Regarding the
Choice and the Freedom of Foods.[12] Zwingli justified this publication
by pointing out his responsibility as pastor, that at a time when a
variety of views on the issue of fasting had arisen, it was his duty to
bring the opinion of the Bible to bear on it. Zwingli, after citing biblical passages, concluded that a Christian may eat all foods because
in themselves they are neither good nor bad; only by abusing them
does a person take harm. Then Zwingli responded in detail to these
four objections: (1) although all foods are permitted to all Christians,
at specific times (therefore during fasting seasons or on Fridays) there
are exceptions to this rule; (2) if one were allowed to eat meat during
fasting season, abstention would no longer be practiced at all; (3)
even though the commandment to fast is a human commandment,
one cannot simply abrogate such a regulation of our pious ancestors;
(4) to eat meat during Lent gives offense to the weak in faith. Zwingli
answered these reservations one by one. No generally valid rule of
food can be derived from the Bible, the "Divine Law," as Zwingli
called it.[13] Salvation does not depend on it. "If you like to fast, do it;
if you don't like to eat meat, don't eat it, but do not touch a Christian's freedom."[14] He declared that to transgress a rule of fasting is not
a sin and therefore could not be punished by the church; it is true that
one should guard against causing annoyance or giving offense, yet the
preacher also has a duty to teach the weak; one should rehearse evangelical freedom, and this freedom experiences limitation only when
a threat of public disturbance exists.[15] Thus Zwingli advocated

relegating the practice of fasting to the private sphere. He concluded by offering to refute objections on the basis of Scripture.

One cannot say that Zwingli based his writing on freedom on Luther's treatise, *The Freedom of a Christian*, with which he was familiar. Zwingli's sermon is noteworthy, on the whole, for the strong logic of its thought process. It has characteristics of a well-planned, precisely formulated scientific treatise. Like Luther's, it deals with the theme of freedom. But whereas the Wittenberger spoke about a Christian's freedom from the law in general, Zwingli applied this dispensation solely to human commandments and regulations; the gospel contains the law of God, which of course must be obeyed. A fundamental contrast to Luther with regard to law and gospel was therefore already discernible in Zwingli's first reformatory writing.

When evaluating his statements, one must, finally, emphasize their measured tone: only monks and religious orders are caricatured and the authority of the scholastic church teacher Thomas Aquinas ridiculed. "Accordingly, they [the defenders of the commandment to fast] come with that Thomas, just as though one single mendicant monk had been given the power to dictate to all Christian people."[16]

Just how far Zwingli had distanced himself from his master Erasmus with this statement regarding any judgment on the ecclesiastical situation is shown by the latter's stance on the subject of a similar violation of the fasting rule in Basel. Erasmus shared the view that fasting rules could not be kept, but demanded that changing or abolishing them be done under the leadership of ecclesiastical princes; as long as the rule existed, it should be obeyed. That is why he took the transgressors sharply to task and condemned their action as a desecration of evangelical freedom. Zwingli, on the other hand, considered the existing practice to be an abuse by ecclesiastical authorities and, in any case, denied them the right to set rules in these matters;[17] this should be the business of individual Christians. Thus Zwingli and Erasmus differed in their assessment of the duties of ecclesiastical authorities and therefore in their concept of church.

During the three weeks that elapsed between the oral lecture and its publication, developments in Zurich were coming to a head. The city Council requested expert opinions on the issue of fasting from the Great Minster chapter and the three people's priests in the city. Their response agreed with Zwingli's opinion that fasting is a practice commanded only by tradition, but at the same time warned against the unregulated abolition of the practice, so as to prevent unrest; thus one should punish transgressions of fasting until a general resolution has been achieved. On the whole, this advice tended toward the position of Erasmus. The Council was requested to urge preachers to make a proclamation to that effect. The commission specifically empowered the Council to deal with this kind of ecclesiastical problem. The Zurich clergy itself thus furthered the disintegration of episcopal authority in favor of the Council.

Constance reacted to the events in Zurich by sending a delegation, which stayed in Zurich from April 7 to April 9, 1522. Zwingli wrote a report of the negotiations.[18] The delegation, characteristically, met with both the spiritual leaders of the city (Great Minster Foundation and the people's priests) and the political authorities in the Small and Large Councils. In their meeting with the government, however, they intended to confine themselves to warnings and admonitions, without entering into any discussions. This plan failed, because the Large Council succeeded in including the people's priests in the meeting, which gave Zwingli the opportunity to appear before the politically decisive governing board of the Large Council as the counterpart of the episcopal curia and to justify his attack on ecclesiastical regulations. Although the Council condemned the violation of fasting both in the concluding agreement with the delegation on April 9, 1522 and in a decree to that effect, it nevertheless added that this was merely an interim decision, since it had demanded that the ecclesiastical authorities furnish a definitive opinion on how one should behave so that "one would not act contrary to the injunctions of Christ."[19]

The significance of this occurrence for further developments can scarcely be overestimated: the Zurich Council assumed responsibility for ecclesiastical matters, recognized Zwingli as the peer of the Constance bishop's appointed representative, and moreover imposed the burden of proof on the ecclesiastical authorities, who were required to justify existing practice on the basis of the Scripture principle. Zwingli could justifiably "report as successful"[20] the outcome of the fasting practice.

Within the Great Minster Foundation, Zwingli was forced to deal with a complaint written by the elegant Canon Hofmann in the spring of 1522. Moreover, a member of the foundation, who remained anonymous, also submitted an indictment. These two reprimands were not echoed in public.

b) Confrontation with the Mendicant Orders

During the post-Easter period, the problem of fasting was followed by the questions of the veneration of saints and the monastic life style as material for conflict. Once again it was radical Zwinglians who started the public controversy by interrupting the sermons of members of religious orders; apparently these members of mendicant orders had expressed their disapproval of Zwingli's criticism of the veneration of saints at the end of June and the beginning of July 1522. Conrad Grebel evidently played a leading role in these disturbances of worship services. The intention was to use these provocative acts to force the city Council to take a more decisive position favoring Zwingli's concepts of reform. But there was as yet no clear majority in favor of Zwingli in the Council, which is why it limited itself to a general prohibition of incitement to unrest without expressing any opinion as to reasons.

A short time later, Zwingli himself seized upon the method of disturbing sermons spectacularly enough by interrupting the traveling mendicant monk from Avignon, Franz Lambert, while he was preaching on Mary and the saints in the Mary Minster. Zwingli called out, "Brother, this is where you err!" This time the purpose was achieved. A disputation involving all the leaders of Zurich was held on the subject of the content of mendicant monks' sermons. As a result of this discussion, the appointed Council delegation directed the monks, on July 21, 1522, to preach scriptural sermons in the manner of Zwingli; they were to proclaim the gospel from that moment on, and to drop scholastics like Thomas and Duns Scotus.[21]

Most recently, Heiko Oberman was justified in stressing the further significant step that this disputation and its consequences represent: for the first time, the political government assumed the function of judge in an ecclesiastical-theological issue and decided it on its own authority. It must be kept in mind, however, that this concerned only the decision of a committee and not the Council as a whole, and that the directive applied only to the mendicant orders. It was in no way a coincidence that the city authorities imposed this regulation on the monasteries, the life style of which they had been trying to bring under control since the fifteenth century. In any case, there can be no question of a general decree requiring preaching in accordance with Scripture.

c) Repudiation of Episcopal Authority

After the episcopal delegation left Zurich, the next step the bishop took, on May 24, 1522, was to write an admonition to the Great Minster and the city government. Naturally, the bishop could not settle the fasting problem in the manner the Council had expected, since this was beyond his powers. Instead, he repeated the traditional position and a general revision of ecclesiastical regulations was not even mentioned.

After this disappointing response, Zwingli and friends from the humanist reform movement felt obliged to take up a further urgent problem of ecclesiastical life. In a petition to the bishop dated July 2, 1522, they demanded the abolition of celibacy — such a burning question for the clergy — and tied their demand to a request that he leave the door open to scriptural (meaning evangelical) preaching.[22] This petition was addressed to the bishop for the sake of appearances, but was intended to bring these problems to the attention of the public and thus serve Reformation propaganda in an effective public relations manner; for this petition was printed within two weeks in appropriate form in German, albeit anonymously, as *A Friendly Petition and Admonition to the Confederates.*[23]

As the title indicates, however, they now addressed secular authorities, and this can be compared to Luther's *Address to the Christian Nobility* of 1520. Their appeal to the Confederate States expressly supported Luther, who in the meantime had been branded a heretic, and appealed to political institutions to permit clerical marriage and to accord wives and children the customary legal protection.

The question of clerical marriage, meanwhile, was no longer an abstract problem for Zwingli himself, since he had been living in secret marriage with a widow of the same age, Anna Reinhard,[24] since the beginning of 1522. The public wedding did not take place until April 2, 1524. Four children were the fruit of this marriage: Regula (1524–1565), William (1526–1541), Huldrych (1528–1571) and Anna (born 1530). Anna did not survive her father; and Zwingli's stepson, Gerold Meyer of Kronau, was killed with him in the battle of Kappel.

Apart from the importance of the celibacy question, the episcopal see's situation was worsened by the fact that the petition had not come just from Zurich but also from pastors of a much wider territory. Furthermore, a distinctly political element had been introduced through the appeal to the Confederates to protect the clergy from the bishop's grasp. The bishop struck back on the same level: in a mandate dated August 10, 1522, he admonished the Zurich government to uphold ecclesiastical order and demanded that they protect the church. Thus the controversy between Zwingli and his ecclesiastical superiors was raised to Confederation level.

The Diet did not react immediately. Instead, Zwingli and his friends were joined by many more common priests. An assembly of clergy in Rapperswil on August 19, 1522, vowed to uphold the Scripture principle. It was in this atmosphere so favorable to himself that Zwingli definitively settled accounts with his local bishop in *The First and Last Word (Apologeticus Archeteles)* of August 22–23, 1522.[25]

In this treatise, Zwingli refuted the episcopal admonition of May 24, 1522 in minute detail, and defended himself above all against the charges of inciting unrest, splitting the church, and heresy. He countered the first accusation by pointing to the actual peace and order prevailing in Zurich as in no other place in the diocese of Constance or in the Confederation. He asserted that the people were in no way being led astray if the issue were to present them with evangelical teaching so that they could leave behind human tradition and ceremonial practices; this kind of preaching could be neither church-divisive nor heretical, since it proclaimed Christ who is the sole foundation of the church. If someone were to demand that ecclesiastical ceremonies should be kept for a while for the sake of good order, one would have to reply that there could be no question of good order in the existing state of the church. Seen as a whole, Zwingli denied the ecclesiastical hierarchy any right to judge matters of gospel proclamation or church order because of their corrupted state. He expected nothing more of his bishop; the bishop was on the side of human law, those wanting reform were on the side of Christ.

Erasmus reacted to this merciless attack with horror.[26] The repudiation of the hierarchy became the mark distinguishing humanist striving for reform from reformatory renewal.

Zwingli's attack of August 1522 can only be understood against the background of the actual revaluation of his position in Zurich after the early summer of 1522. Under the sponsorship of approving Council members, he was surpassing his actual position as people's priest at the Great Minster, and was becoming the trend-setting preacher of Zurich. This development was formally ratified in November 1522 when he was released from specific duties of his office (such as hearing confession and presiding at mass) and expected to devote himself exclusively to preaching. It cannot be determined exactly, however, just how this changed Zwingli's legal position at the Great Minster. In any case, it is certain that the city government as well as the chapter desired this change and instituted it. Whether or not he could therefore be designated "city preacher"[27] who was appointed to an "evangelical parish"[28] remains doubtful. The most likely explanation is that the Council's action was in line with pre-Reformation appointments to preaching offices. In any case, this change in no way warrants the conclusion that the Council definitively reversed itself in favor of Zwingli, which Oberman has justifiably pointed out.[29]

One indication of Zwingli's growing power was the Council's request to him to preach at the Dominican monastery of Oetenbach, although this duty had traditionally been reserved for members of the preaching order.

d) Clarification of the Understanding of Scripture and Veneration of Saints

The treatise *Regarding Clarity and Certainty of the Word of God (Von Klarheit und Gewissheit des Wortes Gottes)*[30] is derived from one of these sermons at the Dominican monastery of Oetenbach. For the first time, Zwingli expressed his opinion, in summary form, of the Scripture principle. His point of departure for the perception of God's Word was taken from anthropological presuppositions: since the essence of human beings is spiritual, in accordance with their being in God's image, human beings really always look up to God; that is why they can comprehend God's Word, which is addressed to this spiritual essence of human beings. God's Word is spiritual and is transmitted not through the text of the Bible, nor through the sermon, nor through church fathers or councils. God the Father himself speaks through his Spirit to a human being; in order to receive him, one has to trust the taking-place of this spiritual connection, pray to receive the Spirit, and abandon one's own reason. The old Adam must be mortified. One can be certain of the Word of God when one feels God's grace and eternal salvation and yet regards oneself as small and futile; the inner self finds pleasure in "the law of God."[31] Someone thus informed is able to understand all the obscure and at first glance contradictory passages of the Bible. No other authority can substitute for the authority of one's own feelings and one's own conscience, for the Word of God, as Spirit, has no other point of contact. The interpretation of the Bible by an ecclesiastical teaching office or by a humanist exegesis no longer has any place in this direct and nonverbal intercourse between God and human beings. Only the person taught by God, the believer, can understand and interpret the Bible.

This tying of the Word of God to inner feeling explains why Zwingli rejected the ecclesiastical hierarchy so vehemently. Their behavior demonstrated how little they had been taught by God. Zwingli held to this conception of the Word of God all his life.

During that same month, a second revised sermon appeared in print: *A Sermon About the Eternally Pure Maid Mary (Eine Predigt von der ewig reinen Magd Maria)*.[32] With this sermon Zwingli obtained a hearing before a wider public on the same topic that had been at issue in his July 1522 controversy with the mendicant monks. There is no doubt that his July 1522 oral criticism of traditional Marian piety was set down here in written form, which was probably the origin of the sermon; that it actually derived from Zwingli's participation in the Einsiedler Feast of All Angels (*Eingelweihfest*) on September 14, 1522 — as is frequently assumed — is scarcely possible, since this would have required its printing within three days.

Zwingli's statements about Mary eschewed polemics and instead served as his defense against the accusation that he had publicly defamed the Mother of God and belittled her reputation. He expressly affirmed the designation "Mother of God" and her eternal and unaltered virginity. What he rejected vehemently, however, was Mary's role as mediatrix of salvation and the religious adoration of her as an individual. He asserted that faith in Christ would be blasphemed against if the reciting of an "Ave Maria" (see Luke 1:28) were imposed as a penance in confession. True honor sees in Mary a model of moral strength, modesty, and firmness of faith. "But if you wish to specially honor Mary, then follow her purity, innocence and firm faith!"[33]

Looking at the events in Zurich from spring to fall 1522 as a whole, it can be noted that precisely the most burning problems of the pre-Reformation church were being discussed at this time: rules of fasting, veneration of saints and of Mary, status of monastic orders, clerical marriage. Their political, economic, social, and human significance was extremely obvious. The key issue was the question of authority: Who decides, on the basis of what authority, and by what criteria? The Scripture principle in the Zwinglian sense rather than that of ecclesiastical tradition was still being applied in Zurich without the Council's official sanction. Relations with the jurisdictional bishop of Constance were strained but not yet broken. Zwingli could in no way be assured of a majority of Council members on his side, but the process of opinion-forming was quite clearly underway. The following two years would bring clarification of his relationship to the bishop and the definitive breakthrough of Zwingli's reformatory ideas.

6. Bibliography

Augustijn, Cornelius. "Die Stellung der Humanisten zur Glaubensspaltung 1518–1530." In *Confessio Augustana und Confutatio. Der Augsburger Reichstag 1530 und die Einheit der Kirche*, 36–48. Reformationsgeschichtliche Studien und Texte 118. Münster, 1980.

Corrodi-Sulzer, Adrian. "Zwinglis Vermögensverhältnisse." *Zwingliana* 4 (1923): 174–88.

Farner, Oskar. "Zwinglis häusliches Leben." In *Ulrich Zwingli. Zum Gedächnis der Zürcher Reformation 1519–1919*, 201–12. Zurich, 1919.

Fast, Heinold. "Reformation durch Provokation. Predigtstörungen in den ersten Jahren der Reformation in der Schweiz." In Hans-Jürgen Goertz, ed., *Umstrittenes Täufertum, 1525–1975. Neue Forschungen*. 2d ed., 79–110. Göttingen, 1975, 1977.

Federer, Karl. "Zwingli und die Marienverehrung." *Zeitschrift für Schweizerische Kirchengeschichte* 45 (1951): 13–26.

Figi, Jacques. *Die innere Reorganisation des Grossmünsterstiftes in Zürich von 1519 bis 1531*. Zürcher Beiträge zur Geschichtswissenschaft 9. Zurich, 1951.

Gäbler, Ulrich. "Huldrych Zwinglis 'reformatorische Wende.' " *Zeitschrift für Kirchengeschichte* 89 (1978): 120–35.

Goeters, J. F. Gerhard. "Die Vorgeschichte des Täufertums in Zürich." In *Studien zur Geschichte und Theologie der Reformation. Festschrift für Ernst Bizer*, 239–81. Neukirchen, 1969.

Locher, Gottfried. "Inhalt und Absicht von Zwinglis Marienlehre." In *Huldrych Zwingli in neuer Sicht*, 127–35. Zurich and Stuttgart, 1969.

Moeller, Bernd. "Zwinglis Disputationen. Studien zu den Anfängen der Kirchenbildung und des Synodalwesens im Protestantismus." *Zeitschrift der Savigny-Stiftung für Rechtsgeschichte* 87 (1970): 275–324; 91 (1974): 213–364.

Nagel, E. *Zwinglis Stellung zur Schrift*. Freiburg i.B. and Leipzig, 1896.

Oberman, Heiko Augustinus. *Werden und Wertung der Reformation. Vom Wegestreit zum Glaubenskampf*. Tübingen, 1977.

―――. *Masters of the Reformation. The Emergence of a New Intellectual Climate in Europe*. Translated by Dennis Martin. Cambridge, 1981.

Pestalozzi, Theodor. *Die Gegner Zwinglis am Grossmünsterstift in Zürich*, H. 1. Schweizer Studien zur Geschichtswissenschaft 9. Zurich, 1918.

Rich, Arthur. *Die Anfänge der Theologie Huldrych Zwinglis*. Quellen und Abhandlungen zur Geschichte des schweizerischen Protestantismus 6. Zurich, 1949.

Stucki, Guido. "Zurichs Stellung in der Eidgenossenschaft vor der Reformation." Ph.D. diss., Zurich, Aarau, 1970.

Vasella, Oskar. *Reform und Reformation in der Schweiz. Zur Würdigung der Anfänge der Glaubenskrise*. 2d ed. Katholisches Leben und Kämpfen im Zeitalter der Glaubensspaltung 16. Münster, 1965.

Walton, Robert C. *Zwingli's Theocracy*. Toronto, 1967.

Wyss, Karl-Heinz. *Leo Jud. Seine Entwicklung zum Reformator 1519–1523*, 3:61. Europäische Hochschulschriften. Bern and Frankfurt, 1976.

V

BREAKTHROUGH IN
ZURICH (1523–1525)

1. The First Zurich Disputation,
January 19, 1523

Events in the summer of 1522 had brought no clarification, for the controversy regarding the same issues continued through the remainder of 1522. There were continual refusals to tithe and violations of the fasting rule. The Council punished these transgressions, but could not wrestle through to a decision on the problem of monasteries.

Inhabitants of the Dominican monastery in Oetenbach — which housed primarily members of influential Zurich families — had split into two factions. One group, influenced by reformatory preaching, wanted to leave the monastery, but this would have had significant financial consequences for their relatives. At the beginning of December, the legal property issues involved forced the city Council to make a decision; but such tumultuous scenes occurred between adherents and opponents of Zwingli that any decision was postponed.

More incisive than these internal signs of unrest was the growing tension between Zurich and the bishop as well as its Confederation partners. As we mentioned before, Zwingli had reached beyond the borders of Zurich to address a wider Confederation public. In *A Divine Admonition to the Confederates in Schwyz*,[1] a tract containing political dynamite, he had appealed to his compatriots in Schwyz to abolish — in accordance with the example of Zurich and for the

good of the fatherland — the blasphemous and unchristian pension
system. In July 1522, the Diet had given its opinion on the church
issue and condemned these new-fashioned teachings in general terms,
undoubtedly aiming at Zwingli and Zurich.

By late 1522, the disagreements became obvious, for in November
the issue of religion in the Common Lordships was discussed at the
Diet for the first time. Complaints against the sermons and the marriage of a pastor friendly to the Reformation had become vocal in the
duchy of Baden. The governing states decided to deliver him to the
episcopal court in Constance. Moreover, the guardians in the
Common Lordships were ordered to inform on pastors supporting
the Reformation.

In contrast to these developments, the Zurich Council was protecting priests from the clutches of the bishop: when the pastor of Höngg
was summoned before the episcopal court for making derogatory
remarks about his spiritual superior, the abbot of Wettingen, he
appealed to the Zurich Council as his secular authority and real judicial authority. The Council in fact took up the case, which caused the
abbot to appeal to the Confederation Diet. The Diet defended the
abbot's spiritual rights and commanded Zurich to stop lending government support to refractory pastors. The Council had clearly acted
in line with Zwingli's *Admonition to the Confederates* of July 13,
1522, although Zwingli's appeal bore no fruit among those he had
really addressed.

Because of these events, the Diet once again took up this ecclesiastical problem on December 15, 1522, and recommended that its Confederation members prohibit the "new" teachings and supervise the
printing of books in Basel and Zurich. This exhortation was equiva-
lent to a strong indictment directed at Zurich, since this Confederate
was being accused of nothing less than harboring treasonable views;
Zurich's behavior could be interpreted as a violation of the spirit of
the alliances. In any case, Zwingli's claim that Zurich was the most
peaceful city in the Confederation no longer held true.

Zurich had meanwhile given up hope of any comprehensive solution to its ecclesiastical problems. Nothing could be expected from
the pope anymore, as was demonstrated in *A Suggestion About How
to Consider the Proposals Hadrian Made at Nürnberg (Suggestio*

deliberandi super propositioned Hadriani Nerobergae facta),[2] Zwingli's opinion of papal proposals made at the Diet of Nürnberg.

In view of the increasingly critical situation in both domestic and foreign affairs at the end of the year, the Zurich Council felt obliged to use its own initiative and find a solution on its own. Concern to uphold public peace and responsibility for protecting its subjects from external attacks were incorporated seamlessly into the existing policies of the Council. But both the form of the arrangement and the disproportionately large expense appear unusual.

On January 3, 1523, the Large Council addressed a so-called Notice[3] to Zurich's clergy in the city and the countryside, inviting them to a meeting in the Zurich courthouse on January 29. The reason given was that dissension had arisen among the preachers. One faction thought it had faithfully preached the gospel, while the other faction called their proclamation heresy and seduction; and this state of affairs continued even though the first faction had declared its willingness to answer these charges. Now was the opportunity for everyone to present their thoughts, based on Holy Scripture, in the German language. In consultation with scholars, the Council would render a decision as to which of the two factions would be permitted to continue their proclamation.

The bishop of Constance was invited to attend in person or to send a representative, but the notice did not assign him a particular role. What the Council had in mind is reminiscent of the July 21, 1522 meeting. Government would judge the content of proclamation in consultation with theological experts. But, in contradistinction to the meeting of the summer of 1522, this invitation was formal and in writing; even the bishop was taken into consideration. Furthermore, the Council, as supreme and ultimate authority, intended to arrive at a definitive judgment. Specifically, the Council was calling upon the clergy living in its territory to present objections to Zwingli's preaching. It reserved to itself the right to judge the validity of these objections; the basis for all discussions was to be Holy Scripture.

Zwingli had offered several times, in writing, to account orally for his sermons;[4] indeed, all his writings of 1522 were really calculated to give an accounting of his activity. Zwingli's offer coincided with the intentions of his most respected opponent Konrad Hofmann. Hofmann, too, had demanded a public debate.[5] But what contradicted the expectations of a theological-academic disputation from the very beginning was that the Council — not scholars or the bishop — chaired the meeting, and there were really no disputation theses available.

Zwingli only helped fill the gap a little by setting up his *Sixty-seven Articles*,[6] because these were not disputation theses at all but rather summary statements of previous sermons. Therefore these *Sixty-seven Articles* or *Concluding Statements* can in no way be considered a "program of the Reformation,"[7] for Zwingli explicitly stated that this is how he had preached.[8]

On the other hand, the *Sixty-seven Articles* do bear the characteristics of an "account of faith." The starting point for all his expositions is the gospel, and thus Zwingli once again pushed the authority problem into the forefront. "All those who say that the gospel is nothing without the protection of the church err and blaspheme God."[9] This strong rejection of the ecclesiastical teaching office defined his parameters. With regard to content, Zwingli determined "the sum of the gospel" to be "that our Lord Jesus Christ, true Son of God, proclaimed to us the will of His heavenly Father and has saved us from death with His innocence and has reconciled us with God. That is why Christ is the only way to salvation for all who ever lived, live, and will live."[10]

Actually, Zwingli summarized his proclamation in an apologetical and polemical manner with the two slogans "by Scripture alone" (*sola scriptura*) and "Christ alone" (*solus Christus*). The claim of Scripture and Christology to possess sole validity was placed in antithesis to the ecclesiastical teaching office and church practices, which gave it its trenchancy. There was no mention of any doctrine of justification (*sola fide*, by faith alone), yet the concept of salvation through Christ alone, as the Second Article of the Creed expressed it, was his basis for every single criticism of the church. Luther's doctrine of justification, with its emphasis on "by faith alone," corresponds to Zwingli's concept of the gospel as the supreme revelation of the will of God. God wills that one listen only to Christ, the Head,[11] for our salvation consists in our faith in him.[12] This is how one learns that doctrines and human teaching are of no use for salvation.[13] If Luther started with the insight that works do not aid salvation, and if for him the human being in the face of God is the focal point of interest, then the Zuricher shared this starting point but was also concerned with how Christians, in accordance with the will of God, must encounter their neighbors, and what the rule of conduct in a Christian community must be.

Zwingli's preaching had an ethical and social-ethical bent. Gottfried W. Locher therefore hit the mark when he said, "Luther sees before him the troubled (*angefochtenen*) human beings and proclaims to them the *solus Christus*, the *Christus pro me* (Christ for me). Zwingli sees before him mendacious and self-seeking human beings and the disruption of their social life."[14] The *Concluding Statements* carried through this basic concern logically, by taking a stand on the burning issues of ecclesiastical and social life. His main themes are: Holy Scripture is supreme guiding principle; Christ's sacrifice on the cross forbids other ways or means of obtaining the forgiveness of sins; all Christians are equal, which is why there can be neither a spiritual authority nor a particular life style for clergy (against celibacy, monastic orders, priestly vestments, oaths); secular government is entitled, and has the duty, to regulate all ecclesiastical and secular matters, as long as it desires to be solely a Christian government. If the government acts outside "Christ's rule of conduct," it can be deposed.[15]

The meeting on January 29, 1523 drew a tremendous crowd. Approximately six hundred participants gathered, almost all of them from Zurich. Despite the lukewarm invitation he had received, the bishop also sent a delegation led by Johannes Fabri. At the bishop's court, the Zurich events had been classified as part of the larger controversy around Luther, and, when it was decided to send a delegation, the meeting was referred to as "a disputation of Ulrich Zwingli in the Luther affair."[16] The deputation was ordered not to take part in any discussion; rather, in accordance with the hierarchy's self-understanding, it was simply to protest against the meeting as a whole and to function as observer. No other outside experts are mentioned as attending.

There is no transcript of the debate; there are only reports by individual participants, which are naturally biased to reflect their respective positions.[17] The authority problem was again at the core of the

morning discussion, in which especially Fabri and Zwingli participated. To Fabri's declaration that an ecumenical council would have
to decide these pending issues, Zwingli countered that this assembly
was a Christian assembly in the sense of the early church, and that
the congregation had a right to judge and did not need a special
teaching authority.

Surprisingly, the city Council already arrived at a verdict during
the noon break. No one had succeeded in proving Zwingli guilty of
heretical statements, and therefore he would be allowed to continue
in his present style until instructed otherwise. Fabri attempted to
grab control by designating Zwingli's theses "in error" and by insisting on the necessity of an ecclesiastical teaching office. It became
obvious at this moment, at the latest, that it had been a tactical error
for him to attend the disputation at all.[18] How could the vicar general
deny the right of the Council and of the assembly to make a judgment in ecclesiastical matters on the one hand, and yet at the same
time enter into a discussion on the contents of these same matters?

In any case, his retreat in this skirmish worsened the bishop's position. The following aspects of the Council's conclusion — the so-called
Dismissal (Abschied)[19] — should be singled out. Specific reference is
made to the quarrels mentioned in the notice, as well as to the bishop's unkept promise of April 9, 1522. For these reasons, "in the name
of God, for the sake of peace and Christian unanimity"[20] they had
taken the matter in hand themselves. All clerics had been given the
opportunity to present possible complaints and accusations, no one
had refuted the Sixty-seven Articles Zwingli had made public, and
that is why he could continue his preaching. All other preachers were
to teach only in accord with Scripture and refrain from slander, or
they would be punished.

Research provides no unanimity about the cause, purpose, procedure, characteristics, or consequences of the meeting. The following
contradictory opinions have been presented.

1. The whole assembly was organized in close agreement between
Zwingli and the Council to manipulate public opinion and as a
demonstration of power. There can be no question of a real
decision.[21]

2. The meeting, although in the mainstream of medieval disputa-

tions and diocesan synods, nevertheless represents something entirely new and is the first city meeting of this kind during the Reformation period. It is a matter of "invention."[22] It is not a matter of an informal religious disputation excluding the question of truth. Since the notice had insisted on the Scriptural principle, the result had already been anticipated and the disputation had been given a kind of "preaching character." Its real purpose was to achieve the city's intention of creating a broad base in favor of the Reformation. On the whole, one could call it the founding assembly of the evangelical church of Zurich.[23] This concept of the church-founding function of the first Disputation was further explained by Oskar Farner, who stated that it was at this time that the "order of the state church" was determined and fixed in written form.[24]

3. Otto Scheib and Heiko Oberman, on the other hand, assign the meeting to the civil-law sphere. As guardian of public order and possessor of the highest juridical power, the Council had stepped in and investigated the slanders and heresies charged against Zwingli. "The Council considered these proceedings to be not an academic disputation but rather clearly a court trial,"[25] which is why "in the concluding report, it was not a question of a 'Reformation mandate' or an 'introduction of scriptural preaching' in the Reformation sense, but rather of a pacification measure."[26]

4. The character of the meeting changed while it was in progress. Although one at first expected an assembly that would sit in judgment over Zwingli, after the repeated intervention of Fabri the "clergy synod" turned into the "first evangelical General Synod" which succeeded "in formulating the assembly's claim to find the truth for the whole Church in such a way that it rescinded the authority of the university [and of the episcopate] as an independent authority, and at the same time ascribed that authority to the Synod."[27]

With regard to these diverse assessments, the following points can be maintained:

1. In view of Zwingli's uncertainty and the haste with which he put together the *Sixty-seven Articles* immediately before the disputation, and in view of the confusion accompanying the preparations, proceedings, and results, any detailed conference beforehand

between Zwingli and the political authorities can be excluded. There is no evidence to show that Zwingli participated in the preparation of the authorities' decisions.

2. Certainly the Council's main concern in the notice was for Zwingli personally. During the course of the debate, its purpose to clear him of the charge of heresy was achieved. To that extent, the disputation had a juridical aspect that Zwingli himself stressed. He later pointed out that he had submitted to a public trial in Zurich and that he had been given the opportunity to defend himself orally against his attackers.[28]

3. By clearing Zwingli, the Council protected existing practice on the one hand, and on the other hand the dismissal transcended any verdict of not guilty, since it ordered preachers to act according to the Scripture principle. Thus the dismissal attained the character of a generally binding government regulation and transcended the framework of the notice. The Council announced its intention to protect all besides Zwingli who preached in the manner of the Great Minster pastor. Thus the dismissal went far beyond the discussion of July 21, 1522. At the same time, this decision in written form assured Zwingli's position as Zurich's trend-setting pastor and implied his role as consultant in future controversies.

4. No direct decisions at all were arrived at with regard to a new church order or eventual reform. The *Sixty-seven Articles* were precisely *not* passed as a "program" by the Council. For this reason one can only speak conditionally of a "church founding."

5. On the other hand, the first disputation prejudiced the interior organization of the Zurich church. It is by no means a coincidence that no move toward founding a church was visible. Zwingli made no spectacular moves at all in matters of church order, because he simply did not attribute any independent organization to the church in the community. Rather, he regarded its order to be a task to be achieved by the Christian civil authority. On the church side, the only thing opposed to this civil authority is the preaching office, as shepherding and guardian office, the duties of which Zwingli would soon describe. This peculiarity of Zwingli's definition of the relationship of church and state, as one would call it today, first became visible in January 1523. That is why Bernd Moeller was correct when he said, "The embedding of the church in the city community rendered

superfluous any effort to create independent church organizational forms that would transcend their duty to safeguard leadership through the word of God; indeed it could have proved a hindrance."[29]

6. Only the future would show how the burning problems summarized by Zwingli in the *Sixty-seven Articles* were solved: the sacrifice of the mass, veneration of saints, fasting rules, monastic life, celibacy, oaths, excommunication, clergy contributions, tithing. In any case, a Council decision was necessary for any change whatever, which necessitated the tedious process of persuading people in every individual case. In Zurich, general solutions had no value.

7. Zwingli regarded councilmen as the legitimate representatives of the Christian community, which is why he acknowledged their right to speak in the name of the church and to make decisions. The government availed itself of this responsibility with its dismissal of the first disputation; Zwinglianism was strongly tied to this principle. Zwingli was shortly to hear the same argument against this principle that he had advanced against the episcopal hierarchy: There were obviously lukewarm and lax Christians among the councilmen; such people could not represent the Christian community; only the truly pious, subject to moral discipline, had the right to make judgments.

8. Seen as a whole, one would have to warn against an overestimation rather than underestimation of the significance of the disputation when looking at these statements made by Zwingli researchers.

2. Theological Development:
Analysis and Reasons for the Concluding Statements

The only concrete measure resulting from the disputation was the Council's announcement of an agreement with the bishop, according to which the Council would assume jurisdiction over all quarrels between clergy and laity in the countryside too. Thus the rural clergy were made equal to their city colleagues, and the Council increased its jurisdiction. Perhaps this measure contributed to the now rapidly increasing number of rural pastors sympathetic to the Reformation. On the other hand, that January 1523 disputation eased the ecclesiastical situation in Zurich for months.

Just as in 1522, however, a variety of provocative actions drew attention to still unresolved issues. Leo Jud, who had meanwhile

obtained the influential pastorate of St. Peter's in Zurich, disrupted
a worship service in the Oetenbach cloister in tried and true fashion.
As a result of this tumult, most of the nuns were able to quit the
order, and members of other convents followed. The same Leo Jud
also interrupted a sermon by the Augustinian prior. Several priests
went public with their marital ties and had public weddings. Zwingli
was not among them; he waited until his first child was underway.

A purified liturgy in German was used in baptismal services at the
Great Minster after August 1523. Statues of saints and icons, called
"idols" by Zwingli adherents, were almost always removed from the
churches in orderly fashion, but sometimes it came to rowdy and
blasphemous scenes. Criticism from the pulpit increased against the
idleness of monastery inhabitants and against canons who lived a
good life at the expense of farmers. The issue of contributions to
ecclesiastical institutions became more urgent.

Zwingli was not in the forefront of all these provocations. Jud, his
closest friend and colleague among the clerics, preached much more
aggressively. Moreover, as in 1522, determined lay people were
demanding the abolition of customs and practices they considered
unchristian. During these months, Zwingli was devoting himself to
writing. He expanded his *Sixty-seven Articles* into a standard treatise,
and expressed his opinion on pending questions in other essays.

The treatise, *Analysis and Reasons for the Concluding Statements
(Auslegen und Gründe der Schlussreden)*[30] is Zwingli's most comprehensive publication, in which he wished to compensate for the
debate on the *Sixty-seven Articles* that had not taken place at the
time they were presented. This intention explains its literary style, as
the treatise is reminiscent of an oral discussion: possible objections are
refuted; opponents ("you papists")[31] are addressed directly; possible
impressions of a neutral observer ("of a simple Christian")[32] are
reproduced. The book contains several other examples.[33] Zwingli
trusted to the power of his argument, because he was convinced he
had the truth of God on his side.[34] He wrote that he had learned from
his own preaching how persistent clinging to God's Word allowed all
objections to fall by the wayside.[35] He started with the conviction that
he was facing an irresolute opponent.

Zwingli now expanded his previously published statements by revealing the theological principles that guided his analysis:

1. A sharp contrast between God and creature traverses all reality, and is not even lifted by Christ's incarnation. The incarnation is governed by God's reconciliation (doctrine of satisfaction). Christ, the Son of God, has by his death on the cross fulfilled the demands of God's righteousness, and has thus liberated human nature from the slavery of sin. From this concept of God Zwingli drew the further conclusion about the comprehensive providence of God and its anthropological corollary: there is no such thing as free will.[36] From the basis of God's spirituality, Zwingli, in impressive and striking fashion, gained his arguments for a polemic he expanded into new areas such as sacrifice of the mass, sacramental forgiveness of sins in confession, invocation of saints, veneration of images. These religious practices must count as deification of creatures and are on the same level as the "false worship" that the Bible so often fights against.[37]

2. Zwingli occupied himself extensively with the nature of sin; it seemed to him to be an irreparable tear in visible nature. The expression he used for it, *prästen*, does not mean any lessening of the depth of sinfulness.[38] Since Christ has liberated human nature from sin, sacramental forgiveness of sin makes no sense. Binding and loosing power is exercised in the proclamation of Jesus' death and therefore in the sermon. Thus Zwingli turned against the traditional doctrine of the power of the keys, and especially against Luther's retention of auricular confession.[39]

3. On the other hand, Zwingli acknowledged the justification of Luther's designation of the Lord's Supper as a "testament." He was not yet preoccupied with the question, later to become so controversial, regarding the bodily presence of Christ in the sacrament. Side by side with Luther, the only issue for him at this time was to refute the sacrificial character of the Lord's Supper and the transformation of the elements (doctrine of transubstantiation). John 6 was the exegetical basis on which he designated the Lord's Supper as a rational/spiritual event. In his presentation of the doctrine of the Eucharist, Zwingli's terminology was quite symbolic with reference to his relationship to Luther.[40] Although he recognized Luther's merit in the struggle against the papal church, he nevertheless correctly emphasized that he had not arrived at his reformatory insights through Luther.

4. In his doctrine of the church, Zwingli differentiated between a

general "catholic" invisible church and the assembly of Christians in one place:[41] Christianity is a hidden spiritual entity which can be represented by neither the pope nor bishops or councils, therefore the Roman church and its hierarchy has no place in this concept. Zwingli rejected a separate spiritual jurisdiction; all clerics should be placed under the jurisdiction of the appropriate civil judicatory;[42] no one need pay attention to excommunication by a bishop; excommunication is the responsibility of the individual congregation. In accordance with his lack of interest in concrete organizational measures, Zwingli ignored the question of how the congregation should carry out the exclusion. There would soon be conflict regarding this point in Zwingli's camp.

5. The detailed contrast between "divine" and "human" righteousness is encountered here for the first time as the basis of ethics and social ethics. Divine righteousness — Zwingli also called it "the law of God" or the "law of nature"— is actualized in the double commandment of love (Matt. 22:37–40). It is a moral claim upon the inner person, yet cannot, in essence, be fulfilled, nor can it be forced. In face of it, all human beings are proved sinners. Contrasted to it is the "lame" human righteousness,[43] the order within a community. It concerns the outer person and is concerned with visible acts and dealings but not with attitude. Civil government has been charged with the administration of human righteousness.

After rejecting a specifically spiritual jurisdiction, Zwingli logically went into detail regarding the rights and duties of government. That is how he attained the basis for his concrete admonitions against rioting and economic exploitation on the part of monasteries and mercantile monopolies. Zwingli remained unaware of Luther's differentiation of law and gospel as a fundamental principle of scriptural exegesis.

These five principles distinguish Zwingli from Erasmus. Nor do they agree with Luther's theology. They express Zwingli's own theological thinking which he would maintain to the end of his life. They are typical of Zwinglianism.

The *Analysis of the Concluding Statements* furthermore clearly revealed the method of argumentation that Zwingli frequently employed. "Step by step" (*per gradationem*)[44] he moved from a general observation to detailed theological statements. For example, in this treatise he derived basic anthropological facts from his concept of God. Zwingli's fundamental thought structure, which we shall encounter frequently, has seldom been traced; Ernst Gerhard Rüsch's essay is one of the first attempts to do so.

Zwingli was already preparing two other essays for publication while he worked on the *Analysis of the Concluding Statements*. His essay *Regarding Divine and Human Righteousness (Von göttlicher und menschlicher Gerechtigkeit)*[45] appeared two short weeks after the *Analysis*. In this essay, Zwingli described the position of government with the aid of his fundamental ethical principle. He had been accused of weakening the authority of civil laws, and these charges were gaining in importance because he was forced to address more far-reaching social and economic demands in his own camp. According to these demands, divine righteousness should be substituted for existing (human) order in church and society; insofar as existing forms of political, civil, and economic life were not explicitly derived from the gospel, the source of divine righteousness, they should be eliminated. That was the reason for objecting to collecting interest and rental fees; this contradiction to the gospel is summarized in government, a judging and punishing authority; a Christian community should instead be based on the law of love.

Zwingli countered with a sharp distinction between divine and human righteousness: experience teaches us that human beings do not obey the law of love, which is why the other commandments are necessary, for they serve to protect the neighbor.[46] This arrangement reverses temporal need and raises "poor" human righteousness; the government's coercion is needed for this purpose. The intention to adopt divine righteousness at this time already is a utopian dream. However, divine righteousness remains the criterion for earthly righteousness, and therefore the best government is the one that brings its laws into line with those of God. Zwingli used sin to justify the existence of a government that calls itself Christian and yet imposes capital punishment. He conceded the usual economic practices, but sharply criticized the everyday abuse of interest payments and the unbearable burden imposed on the farmers. Zwingli asserted that government must prohibit such exploitative practices; farmers should have to pay a capital tax only after a corresponding harvest yield.

There is still a difference of opinion in evaluating this extremely

well-conceived treatise, which is one of the most impressive social-
ethical depositions of the Reformation. Although the general opinion
until the 1930s was that here could be seen the work of the politician
Zwingli, who was a conservative in social matters,[47] increased theological appreciation for the treatise is slowly developing, especially
through the efforts of Arthur Rich. According to him, Zwingli called
attention to the social-ethical responsibility of the Christian, or
rather of the church, in *Regarding Divine and Human Righteousness*. Although Gottfried W. Locher sees in Zwingli's insight its
superiority to Luther's individualistic ethics,[48] others assert that there
is no discernible difference between him and Luther,[49] and even that
Zwingli is at this point directly influenced by Luther.[50] In any case,
any precise clarification of differences or parallels between Luther's
two-kingdom doctrine and Zwingli's expression of double righteousness is still lacking.

Finally, Zwingli, in *An Attempt Regarding the Canon of the Mass
(De canone missae epichiresis)*,[51] drew consequences for liturgy out of
his insight that the mass is not a sacrifice. He perused the texts of the
mass — especially the core texts, the canonical prayers — from this per-
spective, and then made suggestions for alternatives. He could con-
done the use of liturgical vestments and theologically pure Latin
chants; the proposed reformatory worship service was still following
the order of the mass, although this would be dropped two years later
in favor of a new definitive arrangement. Zwingli's cautious
approach caused some to raise objections, which is why he defended
himself in *Defense of the Booklet on the Canon of the Mass (De
canone missae libelli apologia)*,[52] but he nevertheless made some concessions to criticism. Zwingli's work on the liturgy of the mass deep-
ened his conviction that the Lord's Supper is a celebration to recall
the death of Christ. In tone and content *Attempt (Epichiresis)* and
Defense (Apologia) are among Zwingli's harshest anti-Catholic
writings.

3. The Second Zurich Disputation,
October 26–28, 1523

The iconoclastic activities already mentioned above increased in
September 1523. Juridical investigations proved that it was not a

matter of a few isolated incidents. The city Council therefore appointed a committee on September 29, 1523 to work out recommendations with regard to church decorations "and other matters." The committee consisted of eight leading councilmen and the three people's priests (Zwingli, Heinrich Engelhart, and Jud).

The Large Council followed the committee's recommendation to hold a disputation. An invitation to Zurich for Monday, October 26, 1523 was sent out.[53] The differences between it and the notice of the first disputation of January 1523 are remarkable. True, the invitation was again directed chiefly to the clergy in the Zurich territory, but this time it also included lay people — everyone was invited to participate. Furthermore, in addition to the bishop of Constance, the dioceses of Chur and Basel, as well as Basel University, were invited to attend; and finally, the Council also explicitly addressed the twelve other Confederate States. The Council's intention was to make the disputation a Confederation affair.

Since Zwingli had already developed some plans in the summer of 1523,[54] one can assume Zwingli's greater influence on the preparations for the second disputation. The invitation made the purpose of the event perfectly clear: as was known, it had been determined a while ago that only that which was in harmony with Holy Scripture could be preached; according to biblical precepts, church decorations are not permitted; the mass was also being celebrated in ways differing from the one instituted by Christ; quarrels and controversy had arisen on these two issues; the Christian government was, for the sake of peace and reconciliation, inviting everyone to express their opinion for or against these two principles; as a result of the debate, the Council would take the appropriate steps to achieve peace.

The meeting therefore assumed the character of a disputation from its very preconditions. Emil Egli's characterization of a "large exegetical congress" is therefore correct.[55] An official transcript of the three-day disputation was published,[56] which is why documentation is significantly better than for the first disputation. Even more people attended this meeting — probably about nine hundred, including about three hundred and fifty priests. However, official delegates from other judicatories were missing. Neither the bishop nor the Confederate States sent representatives.

Zwingli again bore the brunt of the disputation, this time seconded by Jud. They were opposed by Canon Hofmann, who defended traditional piety; like Fabri at the first disputation, he doubted the authority of the civil government to judge this kind of issue. Hofmann's proposal on procedure demonstrates how much he nevertheless wanted a disputation to take place: all who were present should be asked, one by one, for their position on these two theses. This method had important consequences, for it quickly exposed the clergy's lack of education.

On the first day, "pictures" were discussed. In opposition to Zwingli's rejection of pictorial representations, their pedagogical value was pointed out and the christological argument was advanced that Christ, as human being, should really be made visible in human fashion.[57] Even though these objections to Zwingli were advanced awkwardly, they nevertheless revealed the weak point in his "Nestorian Christology":[58] Zwingli very sharply separated Jesus' divinity from his humanity. The theme of the relationship between divine and human nature would be taken up again in the controversy on the Lord's Supper.

On the second and third days, the dispute was about the essence of the mass, focusing on the conflict regarding its sacrificial character. More important than theological disagreements was a realignment which was meanwhile becoming evident: a public breach between Zwingli and his radical followers. However, at issue was not the mass or images, but once again the authority question. If traditional opponents rejected the authority of the Council because they considered it to be an infringement on the jurisdiction of the ecclesiastical government, then the radicals (especially Konrad Grebel and Simon Stumpf) denied the government's jurisdiction because "the verdict has already been rendered: the Spirit of God judges."[59] In practical terms, this meant that the government cannot even make any law whatever about the removal of images or the alteration of the mass because, since these arrangements are against God, they must stop existing immediately.[60] Zwingli, however, acknowledged the government's right to find the way it deems appropriate to draw consequences from the debate, so that it could proceed "without rebellion."[61]

At this critical juncture, Komtur Schmid of Küsnacht — a small village near Zurich — made a pragmatic suggestion which was adopted.[62] He first noted that evangelical teaching about the uselessness of images had not yet been generally accepted. He therefore suggested that pastors should be ordered, under threat of punishment, to preach about the matter more frequently.[63] Everyone would then recognize that saints and pictures of saints were useless, and the deed would follow on its own. Schmid also recommended the publication of a short summary of evangelical teaching which would be prescribed to the rural pastors as their basis for proclamation: "That one put it [Christian teaching] into one book and send it into the countryside, and command the priests to proclaim these things."[64] According to Schmid, a difference in development was visible between city and country; although such instruction was no longer necessary in Zurich itself, rural clergy still had to be prepared for these changes — a telling example of the pace-setting role of the city in the adoption of the Reformation. In conclusion, Schmid appealed to the government to accept its responsibility. Schmid thus clearly rejected the radicals and remained on Zwingli's side. An inherent opposition between Zwingli and Schmid, as has at times been asserted in the research literature,[65] did not exist; Schmid merely advised postponing organizational measures.

Around November 1 — the exact date is unknown — the Council passed ordinances in line with Schmid's motion: for the time being, images in the church should be kept, but no new ones should be added; only the donors had permission to remove their own donations; the order of the mass also would be maintained; and slander would be punished severely. Nevertheless, these two decrees were of a temporary nature, for it was hoped that a definitive decision could be arrived at soon. The Scripture principle was again enjoined, and a short introduction into Christian teaching was announced. In conclusion, it was announced that a few pastors would travel around as "wandering preachers" to support the proclamation of the gospel. Zwingli, Schmid, and Wolfgang Joner (abbot of the Cistercian monastery of Kappel) undertook such a preaching tour in that same month.

During the middle of November, the previously announced booklet and a new ordinance were already being distributed to the Zurich clergy. The following January, the Council also sent it to the clergy and political authorities of the other Confederate States it had invited to the disputation. Zwingli had written the booklet in a few days, and the Council had approved its contents. Thus the *Short Christian Introduction (Kurze, christliche Einleitung)*[66] cannot count as merely a private statement by Zwingli. Rather, the Zurich Council fixed the doctrine in binding form, and therefore the *Short Christian Introduction* is a "public confessional writing of the Zurich Reformation."[67] However, Zwingli did not give a summary of his teaching; instead, he confined himself to a few points, and thus stated what, in his opinion, was at issue in the reformation of the church.

The booklet is divided into two parts. In the first, theoretical part, Zwingli dealt with sin, law, abolition of the law, and gospel.[68] He then addressed the two relevant issues of the mass and of images, but did not go beyond what had already been said.[69] The heart of this booklet is the passage about "the abolition of the law."[70] Zwingli distinguished a threefold liberation from the law, as it "now" occurs:[71] (1) priestly pomp and church splendor are being eliminated; (2) papal doctrine and regulations claiming to secure salvation (like fasting, indulgences, commissioned masses) are no longer valid; (3) the human being who trusts and relies on God is also free from punishment for sin, and this freedom is demonstrated by a humble and virtuous life style. Quite a few people do turn away from ecclesiastical pomp and from papal regulations, but do not alter their innermost life. For Zwingli, therefore, "reformation" is introduced first of all as liberation from useless practices and prescriptions, and a social-moral improvement of the people is expected from it. In conclusion, Zwingli sharply attacked a false understanding of "freedom from law": Christians cannot escape obedience to the secular government; whoever demands disobedience belongs among the "most dangerous enemies of God's teaching."[72] Zwingli thus saw two dangers in the carrying out of the Reformation: no social-moral renewal, and the death of civil order.

With regard to the significance of the second disputation, the following can be noted: (1) Zwingli and his friends left the meeting having once again gained strength. The Large Council had protected both the presuppositions and the content of their proclamation. From then on, the issue in Zurich was no longer whether the traditional church was null and void; only the timing of its dissolution was in question. (2) The role of the government was reaffirmed, as was Zwingli's. As J. F. Gerhard Goeters correctly remarked, "The tendency of government to regulate the church is obvious."[73] (3) Future contours of the Zurich church structure were becoming easier to delineate. The clergy, especially in the countryside, was assigned a key task in order to carry out the will of the state. It was by no means a coincidence that Zwingli preached about the office of ministry on the last day of the disputation.[74] The survey taken at the disputation anticipated the later grading of evangelical clerics at Zurich synod meetings, at which every pastor was very closely examined. The attention the state paid to the clergy in connection with the second disputation became part of the attempt, noted elsewhere, to make the ministry obedient to the state's interests.

4. Political Threat and Theological Maturing (1523–1525)

a) Reluctant Ecclesiastical Renewals

Neither the second Zurich disputation itself nor Zwingli's *Short Christian Introduction* changed things. Nevertheless, traditional practices of piety did abate noticeably after the winter of 1523–24. Church feast days were no longer celebrated, processions were stopped, fasting practices disappeared, and liturgical services were replaced by preaching services.

In December 1523, the Council had set a deadline of Pentecost 1524 for a solution to the problem of eliminating the mass and images. Again with the participation of Zwingli, a commission prepared the resolution to be passed. In a formal opinion, *Proposal Concerning Images and the Mass (Vorschlag wegen der Bilder und der Messe),*[75] Zwingli repeated his well-known views, but did not urge an immediate, general abolition. The Council passed a finely graduated resolution: alteration of the mass was again postponed, as it had been in December 1523. A distinction between city and country was made with regard to images. The Council ordered the removal of images, crucifixes, statues, and murals in the city of Zurich, but each rural congregation was granted the right to remove them on the basis of a majority decision.

During the second half of 1523, the Council resolution was indeed obeyed in the city of Zurich, and church decorations were destroyed under government supervision. Rural parishes followed suit. However, this brought about tumultuous scenes in the parish of Stammheim (northeast of Zurich) because legal removals in the town itself were followed by iconoclastic excesses in the neighboring communities which were under Confederation administration.

Finally, the structure of foundations and monasteries was not only criticized but also thoroughly reformed in spiritual as well as economic respects. This development later led to the dissolution of monasteries, which will be described later.

b) Local Currents of Opposition in Zurich

The cautious action of Zwingli and the government was too slow for the radicals, who had already spoken up at the second disputation. According to them, these proceedings were in direct contradiction to Holy Scripture and they announced a split from Zwingli. This development is a part of the prehistory of Anabaptism.

Local Catholic opposition in Zurich was still concentrated around the Great Minster and around Canon Hofmann. This is where, after the exclusion of the mendicant orders, minds clashed most vehemently. Whereas a number of chaplains in Zwingli's camp at the Great Minster refused to read mass any longer by December 1523, colleagues around Hofmann defended traditional worship. The retired canon moreover accused the Council of procedural errors at the two disputations; he demanded another disputation on the justification of ecclesiastical innovations without the consent of the whole church; and he insisted on the appointment of academic umpires, in accordance with the model of the Leipzig disputation with Luther in 1519.

The Council ignored the last point, but did set up a discussion at which Hofmann and his four followers could present their complaints against the people's priests Zwingli, Engelhart, and Jud before a commission consisting of six councilmen and six Zurich theologians.

This meeting, on January 13 and 14, 1524, can scarcely be called a "third Zurich disputation," because it distinguished itself from both the foregoing almost public meetings with respect to the deciding authority as well as the group of disputants. The discussion was instead patterned after the debate of July 21, 1522. Only this time the role of plaintiff had been reversed: Zwingli was forced to defend himself. He succeeded in doing so without too much effort, and the whole affair looked like a rehearsed exercise. In any case, on January 19, 1524 — probably on the recommendation of the commission to that effect — the Council observed laconically that the five plaintiffs had accomplished nothing, and that they should obey the government mandates; as for the rest, "they can believe what they wish."[76] If they refused to obey these rules, they would be deported from the city. Hofmann himself suffered the consequences and left Zurich. With his departure, the opposition of pastors hostile to the Reformation was definitely broken.

The Constance bishop tried one last time to assume control in Zurich. Regarded as a formal response to the *Short Christian Introduction*, the episcopal publication *Christian Instruction (Christlich Unterrichtung)*[77] dealt with questions of the mass and the cult of images in detail. At the request of the Council, Zwingli wrote Zurich's official rebuttal, *Christian Response of the Mayor and Council of Zurich to Bishop Hugo (Christlich Antwort Bürgermeisters und Rats zu Zurich an Bischof Hugo)*,[78] which repeated the well-known positions. As he had already done when writing the *Short Christian Introduction*, Zwingli personally functioned as theological and church-political consultant to the Council. This written exchange in the summer of 1524 severed all official ties between Zurich and the bishop.

c) The Confederate States' Intervention

The Confederate States had not reacted to Zurich's invitation to attend the second disputation; nor did the dissemination of the *Short Christian Introduction* call forth a direct response from them. This semblance of inactivity was deceptive, for Zurich was not even invited to the meeting of the Diet on January 4, 1524. The twelve states intended to settle their complaints against their fellow Confederate on their own. In essence, the Diet concerned itself with three charges: the Zurich government allegedly shielded Reformation propaganda and excesses in Confederate territories; slanderous speeches against Catholic dogma and piety went unpunished; legal prosecutions of agitators were being obstructed. This obstructionism seemed to the Confederate States to be a particular threat: in one case, peasants had banded together and prevented the arrest of an insubordinate pastor (the so-called Weininger affair). The Diet decided to send a committee of Confederate politicians to Zurich to intervene there.

The charges presented on February 25, 1524 boiled down to a single accusation: Zurich is the seedbed of hatred and discord in the Confederation, and Zwingli and Jud are its ringleaders. The Zurich government promised to investigate, thus choosing delaying tactics.

Tensions increased when Klaus Hottinger, the iconoclast banned from Zurich, was executed in Lucerne in March 1524. Another session of the Diet was convened in April in Lucerne at which representatives of the bishops of Constance, Basel, and Lausanne complained about the violation of ecclesiastical authority by the Reformation movement. In politically adept fashion they prophesied the weakening of civil order too. (Zwingli would later refute this dangerous accusation with the famous argument that the Reformation in no way impaired the authority of secular laws.[79]) At the same time, the ecclesiastical delegation asked the Confederation to provide effective protection against reformatory incursions.

At this session of the Diet, Zurich firmly defended its existing political program. Reaction to these two positions covered a wide range of opinions: Schaffhausen unreservedly took Zurich's side; the other states wanted either to admit evangelical preaching—without, however, initiating ecclesiastical changes (like Berne and Solothurn)—or to fight reformatory awakening with all available means (like the Interior States). In any case, Zurich achieved one political success, since the Confederates declared they had no unfriendly intentions against Zurich at all.

The front against the Reformation was crumbling. Thereupon the firm opponents to any ecclesiastical restructuring banded together in defense against the Reformation in "The Agreement of Beckenried" on April 8, 1524. Zwingli, of course, criticized this alliance.[80]

The removal of church decorations and the events at Stammheim increased the bitterness of the Catholic Confederates. When the Confederate authorities set out to capture one of the Stammheim ringleaders they set off a riot that ended in an attack on the Carthusian monastery of Ittingen. This signified rebellion and disturbance of the peace; the Confederate states demanded that Zurich deliver the ringleaders to them, since they claimed supreme judicial authority in this district. Zwingli warned against such a step, but the Zurich Council handed over — albeit reluctantly — the three ringleaders (two guardians and one pastor) to the Confederate court. Their trial in Baden ended on September 23, 1524, resulting in death sentences for all three.

For Zwingli, who had testified as an expert,[81] and his followers this amounted to a miscarriage of justice. They asserted that the punishment had not been for insurrection but for confessing the reformatory faith. In Zurich the three men were compared to early Christian martyrs, which only aggravated the Confederates' prejudice against Zurich. They regarded the Reformation as a chain of violations of the law. Reactions became more and more irritated on both sides, so that there was fear of war in the Confederation by the fall of 1524.

d) Theological Growth: The Commentary

If one surveys Zwingli's theological statements after his *Analysis of the Concluding Statements*, the following emphases can be recognized. Zwingli established the foundation of his doctrine of society with *Regarding Divine and Human Righteousness*. Continuing social and economic unrest allowed him to state his position again in *Whoever Causes Unrest (Wer Ursache gebe zu Aufruhr)*.[82] Jerome Emser, the Saxon theologian who had also crossed swords with Luther, wrote a defense of the mass against Zwingli's *De canone missae epichiresis (Attempt)*. Zwingli responded with the comprehensive *Objection to Jerome Emser (Adversus Hieronymum Emserum antibolon)*.[83] In connection with the problem of the mass, Zwingli directed his attention to the question regarding the character of the sacrament in general. He found clarity in late 1524 when he discovered his own conception of the Lord's Supper, which has been labeled "symbolic interpretation."

In interaction with practical changes in Zurich, the issue was to determine the status and duties of the civil government and of ecclesiastical officials. In this respect it was easier, according to Zwinglian concepts, to speak about government than about the church. During the second disputation, when it had become evident that pastors carried the main burden of church renewal, Zwingli had preached about their responsibility. The sermon, extensively revised, appeared in print in March 1524.

In 1525, Zwingli produced a revised summary of his theological thinking as a theological-dogmatic companion piece to the institutional consolidation of the Zurich Reformation: *Commentary About the True and the False Religion (Commentarius de vera et falsa religio ie),*[84] which ended his period of transition. Since Zwingli's positio i on social problems and his conception of sacrament will be mentioned in other connections, we can at this point limit ourselves to a characterization of *The Shepherd* and *The Commentary.*

Although the core of the treatise *The Shepherd*[85] is derived from Zwingli's sermon to his ministerial colleagues, its published form no longer addressed them. Zwingli presupposed a position on the part of clerics that no longer existed in Zurich at this time: a hostile secular or spiritual government that threatens reformatory preaching. But this situation did apply especially to the Common Lordships in March 1524. Moreover, the first actual defensive moves by the Catholic Confederates were being made at that time. In any case, Zwingli turned his attention to the Confederation in his book. Accordingly, *The Shepherd* was dedicated to an Appenzell pastor.

Zwingli adeptly compared the "good" with the "false" shepherd, using many images drawn from the Bible.[86] Of course he identified the Catholic office holders as "false" shepherds. The marks of a true shepherd, he asserted, are fearless preaching, a personal life above reproach, championing the poor. In ever new approaches, Zwingli hammered away at the essential duties of a pastor: to expose the corrupt self-interested behavior of the mighty — and the resultant damage to human coexistence — without regard to their position or reputation. This image fit Zwingli's understanding of Reformation: abolition of human commandments and decrees, emphasis on morality. Zwingli affirmed the right of a congregation to depose a "false" shepherd by majority vote or, if that proved to be impossible, to boycott his proclamation.[87]

Although the *Commentary* is a systematic-dogmatic work, neither its intended audience nor its date of writing should be ignored when evaluating it. Zwingli dedicated it to the French king Francis I. He expected French scholars, particularly those at the Sorbonne, to examine his treatise.

His focus of attention on France and on the University of Paris, which was considered the stronghold of Catholicism, was not a public relations gambit. The writing reflected this context. As the title suggests, the "Commentary" is dominated by the contrast between true and false religion. More than he had ever done before, Zwingli placed the pope into the center of his characterization of Catholicism, the "false" religion: as "man of sin" (2 Thess. 2:3), the pope is the antichrist,[88] and therefore the embodiment of the false religion that sets its hopes on something other than on Christ;[89] this is what gave rise to the misery of peoples; it is the duty of secular rulers to provide redress; in Germany, this was already being done. Zwingli now desired to reach out to France with neighborly responsibility.[90]

Zwingli considered himself the equal of Erasmus, his outmoded predecessor, and of Luther. His characterization of the Wittenberg reformer conforms to his own ideal: Zwingli spoke of "great men . . . the presently so very brilliant and successful authors who, it seems to one, have given the world a new face and helped it out of coarseness into morality."[91]

The ways of Zwingli and Erasmus diverged when it came to judging the ecclesiastical hierarchy.[92] Zwingli's wide-ranging goals explain his de-emphasis of polemical elements. In accordance with his favorite writing style, making comparisons, Zwingli's concern was still to refute and reject traditional doctrine and cult. He stressed the positive description of "true" religion, and this again revealed his theological principles mentioned above. His distinction between flesh and spirit, which engage in an "eternal battle,"[93] once again took precedence over everything else. Starting with the theory of satisfaction, Zwingli explained in greater detail and with more precision the appropriation of salvation. A road to salvation (*ordo salutis*) in clear time gradations can be discerned.[94] In the face of God's will, established in his law, human beings acknowledge their desperate situation (self-understanding). In their hopelessness they flee to God's compassion as it is revealed in Christ's saving act; this hope for Christ is accompanied by the will and desire to change.[95] Zwingli tied the experiencing of salvation to moral change, yet left no room for human cooperation. He emphatically underlined the exclusive "pull of the Father" (referring to John 6:44), and thus vehemently rejected free will in his argument with Erasmian humanism.[96] According to him, false religion places its trust in religious activities such as the sacrifice of the mass, veneration of saints, ecclesiastical customs, or in one's own achievements (works righteousness); such a religion is materialistic.

Two sections stand out for their great length when reading the twenty-nine chapters: "Regarding government"[97] and "Regarding the Eucharist."[98] In advance of the Peasants' War, Zwingli understandably defended himself strongly against the prevalent accusation that the Reformation created disorder and licentiousness. He asserted that only the opinion of the Anabaptists brought about these results and that "true" religion supported government and provided it with moral principles; and that a Christian government is the best guarantor of the people's well-being.[99]

The section on the Eucharist mirrored Zwingli's satisfaction and pride in having found the correct understanding of the sacrament. He found a new meaning revealed to him even in the heart of traditional piety. According to Zwingli's unshakable conviction, his interpretation of the Eucharist fit seamlessly into the rest of his theological thinking and agreed with his view of the Bible and early Christianity. The great length of these sections can be explained only by Zwingli's consciousness of having made an essential contribution to the renewal of Christendom with his doctrine of the Eucharist.

5. Bibliography

Courvoisier, Jaques. *Zwingli als reformierter Theologe*. Translated by Rudolf Pfisterer, 11. Zeugen und Zeugnisse. Neukirchen, 1966.

Demandt, Dieter. "Zur Wirtschaftsethik Huldrych Zwinglis." In *Beiträge zur Wirtschafts- und Sozialgeschichte des Mittelalters. Festschrift für Herbert Helbig zum 65. Geburtstag,* 306–21. Cologne and Vienna, 1976.

Eisinger, Walther. "Gesetz und Evangelium bei Huldrych Zwingli." Ph. D. diss., Heidelberg, 1957.

Farner, Alfred. *Die Lehre von Kirche und Staat bei Zwingli.* Tübingen, 1930. Reprint. Darmstadt, 1973.

Gestrich, Christof. *Zwingli als Theologe. Glaube und Geist beim Zürcher Reformator.* Studien zur Dogmengeschichte und systematischen Theologie 20. Zurich and Stuttgart, 1967.

Kläui, Paul. "Notizen über Gegner der Reformation in Zürich." *Zwingliana* 6 (1938): 574–80.

Locher, Gottfried W. *Die Theologie Huldrych Zwinglis im Lichte seiner Christologie.* Part 1, *Die Gotteslehre.* Studien zur Dogmengeschichte und systematischen Theologie 1. Zurich, 1952.

―――. "Grundzüge der Theologie Huldrych Zwinglis im Vergleich mit derjenigen Martin Luthers und Johannes Calvins." In *Huldrych Zwingli in neuer Sicht,* 173–274. Zurich and Stuttgart, 1969.

Moeller, Bernd. "Die Ursprünge der reformierten Kirche." *Theologische Literaturzeitung* 100 (1975): 642–53.

―――. "Zwinglis Disputationen. Studien zu den Anfängen der Kirchenbildung und des Synodalwesens im Protestantismus." *Zeitschrift der Savigny-Stiftung für Rechtsgeschichte* 87 (1970): 275–324; 91 (1974): 213–364.

Muralt, Leonhard von. "Zwingli als Sozialpolitiker." *Zwingliana* 5 (1931): 276–96.

Neuser, Wilhelm H. *Dogma und Bekenntnis in der Reformation: Von Zwingli und Calvin bis zur Synode von Westminster.* In Carl Andresen, ed., *Handbuch der Dogmen- und Theologiegeschichte,* 2:167–238. Göttingen, 1980.

Oberman, Heiko Augustinus. *Werden und Wertung der Reformation. Vom Wegestreit zum Glaubenskampf.* Tübingen, 1977.

Ozment, Steven E. *The Reformation in the Cities. The Appeal of Protestantism to Sixteenth-Century Germany and Switzerland.* New Haven and London, 1975.

Pestalozzi, Theodor. *Die Gegner Zwinglis am Grossmünsterstift in Zürich.* Schweizer Studien zur Geschichtswissenschaft 9. Zurich, 1918.

Pfister, Rudolf, "Kirche und Glaube auf der Ersten Zürcher Disputation vom 29. Januar 1523." *Zwingliana* 13 (1973): 553–69.

Rich, Arthur. "Zwingli als sozialpolitischer Denker." *Zwingliana* 13 (1969): 67–89.

Rüsch, Ernst Gerhard. "Eine Weihnachtsansprache Zwinglis." *Theologische Zeitschrift* 32 (1976): 360–72.

Scheib, Otto. *Die theologischen Diskussionen Huldrych Zwinglis. Zur Entstehung und Struktur der Religionsgespräche des 16. Jahrhunderts.* In Remigius Bäumer, ed., *Von Konstanz nach Trient. Beiträge zur Geschichte der Kirche von den Reformkonzilien bis zum Tridentinum. Festgabe für August Franzen*, 395–417. Munich, Paderborn, and Vienna, 1972.

Stauffer, Richard. *L'influence et la critique de l'humanisme dans le "De vera et falsa religione" de Zwingli*. In *Interprètes de la Bible*, 87–102. Paris, 1980.

Walton, Robert C. *Zwingli's Theocracy*. Toronto, 1967.

Zimmermann, Günter. *Die Antwort der Reformatoren auf die Zehntenfrage. Eine Analyse des Zusammenhanges von Reformation und Bauernkrieg*, 3:164. Europäische Hochschulschriften. Frankfurt am Main and Berne, 1982.

VI
CHURCH REORGANIZATION
(1524–1526)

1. Reformatory Movement and
Social Situation

a) Social and Political Shifts

Our sketch of the development of the Zurich reformatory movement up to this point reveals the decisive part played by the government in the breakthrough of the Reformation. However, there are no
available sources describing the circumstances under which the decisions were made. No minutes were kept at the debates, there are no
lists of participants, there is not even a record of how large a majority
voted for the decisive measures. Therefore there is no way of telling
which particular members of either the Small or the Large Council
were favorably disposed toward the Reformation. One clue to their
identity can be found in the ordinances (and delegations) in the commissions, because the political leadership can be derived from them.

In his pioneering research, Walter Jacob investigated the family,
guild, social, and economic background of sixty-five leading legislators. He then picked out their intensity and manner of political effectiveness, namely, their legislative activity between 1519 and 1528, and
finally, he related these results to the attitude of these individuals
toward the Reformation. Jacob drew the following conclusions: as in
other late medieval cities, the socio-economic elite determined the
political destiny of Zurich. The leading legislators were recruited
almost exclusively from this stratum; in addition, there were a very

small number of social climbers and special cases — legislators from the clergy rolls, particularly the three people's priests, Zwingli, Heinrich Engelhart, and Leo Jud. A comparative study of these politicians proves that no specific characteristic can be discerned that would be decisive in determining membership in the ruling class.

Until 1525, one did not have to be rich, nor belong to a particular guild, nor be of a good family, nor be a certain age, nor be Zwingli's friend in order to play an influential political role in Zurich. Only after 1525 did adherence to the Reformation become important. The reformatory breakthrough in Zurich was not encouraged by a specific social class, nor did it assist a specific group to power; not even the clergy gained greater influence. Seen as a whole, it was a picture of great political and social stability.

But a few things must be made more precise in this comprehensive framework: the influence of the rich people of independent means, already diminishing before the Reformation, was now eroding at a faster pace, so that they had completely disappeared from the political stage by the end of the 1520s. The opponents to the Reformation had a disproportionately large representation in this class. This development was accompanied by the increasing power of the guild leadership.

As an umbrella organization over the individual guilds, so to speak, the chief guild masters or top masters supervised craft regulations. The constituent membership in this committee of three demonstrated a large measure of stability, since only one of the three men was replaced annually, and reelection was the rule. Soon there were actually four top masters, of whom one always withdrew from office. The increasing importance of these four men became evident first by the number of top masters among the leading city legislators and second by the fact that it became customary to delegate mayors and top masters to deal with political matters jointly. This evolved into a parliamentary agency not juridically defined and outside traditional constitutional structures.

This guiding group of six men was clearly given more and more power. It examined incoming news and prepared the responses, sometimes in conjunction with the Small or the Large Council. Above all, either at the specific request of councilmen or with their unspoken agreement, it undertook the selection and nomination of legislators. Although this committee theoretically had no power to enact important legislation, since it remained dependent on the agreement of the Councils, it nevertheless attained a key position with regard to preparation, consultation, and decisions on political affairs.

This group of mayors and top masters consisted almost exclusively of men well disposed to the Reformation, which decisively influenced the breakthrough of the Reformation. The Zurich Reformation owed its political existence to this group of leaders. The reasons for the politicians' friendly attitude to Zwingli cannot be illumined any further.

As in other cities dominated by guilds, the Reformation received greater support in the Large Council than in the Small Council. This can be seen, for example, in the events surrounding the visit of the Constance episcopal delegation in April 1522. Another notable sign is that on January 11, 1524, the Large Council took over from the Small Council the authority to judge sermons. This measure was not rescinded until August 1527, after the opponents to the Reformation and the aristocratic pension receivers — among them Jacob Grebel, who was executed on October 30, 1526 — had been eased out.

b) Social-Political Demands and
Zwingli's Position

With regard to the pending economic issues, a rearrangement of the systems of interest and tithing was at stake. On the matter of interest, Zwingli advocated an interest rate of no more than 5 percent for cash loans. He recommended an amount of interest for real estate dependent on revenue: the risk of a failed harvest should be borne by both investor and recipient of capital. Zwingli had already encountered the tithing problem at the beginning of his activity in Zurich, when he had discussed the traditional system of tithing. Under the influence of his sermons criticizing the church, congregations had already considered their contributions to ecclesiastical authorities headquartered in the city to be a sign of their dependence and a restriction of their autonomy. They felt the local community was being estranged from money. That is why demands for the abolition of tithing were allied with demands for local self-government — most concretely expressed in the election of a pastor by the local congregation. Naturally the congregation would have to provide for his financial support. Thus the fight of the congregations for the abolition of tithing can be placed in the wider context of the liberation of rural congregations from city guardianship. The tithing question is therefore concerned with more than the problem of a church contribution.

Congregations attached to the Great Minster Foundation had already refused to pay the tithe as early as 1522; and in June 1523, six rural congregations explicitly demanded that the Council abolish it, since this payment did not agree with Scripture and the money was being used for idle purposes—this was a barb aimed at the alleged high living of the Great Minster canons. Zwingli defended tithing at this point, in *Regarding Divine and Human Righteousness*, as an institution by human right, as was mentioned above; existing laws could not simply be discarded. This led to a new quarrel between Zwingli and his radical followers. The radicals wanted an unconditional elimination of the tithe, "the cornerstone of a corrupt religious structure."[1]

It was correct to criticize the practice of tithing from the viewpoint of the Bible, Zwingli explained one year later in *Whoever Causes Unrest (Wer Ursache gebe zu Aufruhr)*.[2] He added that the whole economic system, which relied on agreements and contracts, could not be overthrown overnight, however, as the radical hotheads demanded; contributions should be made under the aspect of human righteousness; an instant rearrangement of the economy would create turmoil.[3]

Zwingli advocated a slow, step-by-step procedure to regain the original purpose of the tithe: payment to support the poor and to pay the preacher. One should try to buy up tithing obligations owed to a layman; those to foundations and monasteries would cease of themselves, since these institutions would slowly die out, as was being demonstrated by the Zurich experience.[4] Although Zwingli conceded the relative rights of tithing, he again most harshly condemned economic practices like monopoly, money trading, and currency devaluation, which made him no different from other contemporary critics.

Zwingli blamed these bad conditions on the papacy (he called it "disorder" [*Missordnung*][5] and on greedy "gentlemen." He declared that the common man had already accepted the gospel, but the mighty gentlemen had not;[6] they should recant before divine punishment overtook them.[7] That is why Zwingli, as he had done before, addressed them in particular. This consciousness of the imminent judgment of God, to whom accounts must be rendered, was the requisite framework for Zwingli's concrete suggestions for reform. At the same time, like his contemporaries, he expected a turn for the better to occur first of all through a change of attitude on the part of the secular rulers.

In this treatise, Zwingli primarily addressed readers outside Zurich who were already experiencing the unrest in the rural population which was to lead to the so-called Peasants' War of 1525. Zurich was hardly touched by this movement. Here there were incidents of refusal to pay tithes in several villages, and there were public statements of dissatisfaction with the domination of the city. There were no armed gangs of peasants being formed, but Zurich villages did use orderly legal means to apply to the Council for changes in similarly worded petitions. The demands were for the abolition of the last traces of serfdom, free hunting and fishing, the right to elect pastors, curtailment of tithes, the use of church property to support the poor, enforcement of the prohibition against enlistment as mercenaries, and against pensions. They appealed explicitly to the gospel in their petitions. Zwingli's fine distinction between divine and human righteousness was evidently not being followed.

In May 1525, the Council sought the expert opinion of the people's priests on the peasant petitions[8] and, on the basis of their suggestions, abolished serfdom. A decision on tithes and the problems connected to them was postponed; Zwingli gave his expert opinion on the subject once more.[9] Finally, in August 1525, the Council decided, in accordance with Zwingli's opinion, that rejecting the tithe cannot be justified on the basis of Holy Scripture, since property and signed contracts must be respected; therefore they alleviated the burden of tithing somewhat, but not as much as had been demanded, and existing regulations for the election of pastors remained in force. The Zurich Council nipped all moves toward autonomy in the bud by pointing unmistakably to the obedience due government in accordance with Romans 13. The Council was allowing nothing to undermine the inherent dependence of the rural congregations.

In any case, if one ignores the roots of Anabaptism connected to the Peasants' War, the war bypassed Zurich and did not cause great upheaval or have far-reaching consequences there.

When evaluating Zwingli's social-political statements, one can be certain of the following:

1. According to Zwingli, concrete political, economic, and social conditions must be tested by the criterion of Holy Scripture, "divine righteousness." This is where Zwingli is distinguished from Luther.

2. Even under conditions of clear abuse, changes should be made only step by step and with caution, within the framework of the legal system, since existing obligations, agreements, and contracts the government has agreed to guarantee must be honored. The tithe belongs to the realm of human righteousness. Secular government is responsible for the practice of it, since a spiritual jurisdiction can no longer exist.[10]

3. The Council's interventions in economic life, motivated by the reformatory movement, had not brought the peasants any decisive political or economic relief. That is why it is not surprising that Anabaptists, who were especially concerned to achieve congregational autonomy, should be quite successful. Peasants obliged to make contributions did not care whether they had to pay a monastery or a Council agency. They had no say in the spending of that money in any case.

4. The Council's interest in a close and central supervision of the clergy, which had already become apparent at the second Zurich disputation, was once again becoming evident. Unfortunately, no one has yet researched Zurich clergy in the sixteenth century, so that a sure judgment regarding the clergy's role in Council politics cannot be made. All signs point to the fact that the city government made great efforts to systematically acquire all the powers having to do with the education, selection, installation, and dismissal of pastors, in order to be able to use them as dependable liaison between government and its subjects.

5. In any case, on the whole, Zwingli's preaching and reform activity did not make any immediate incursion into the general political, economic, and social development of Zurich. In summary, the most one can say is that the Council increased its power, since — after

easing out ecclesiastical authorities like bishop and monasteries — it arranged, supervised, and regulated a greater segment of social as well as private life.

2. Dissolution of Monasteries and Welfare Measures

With the year 1525, the Great Minster and the Mary Minster Foundations, as well as the settlements of mendicant orders, ceased to exist in Zurich in their traditional form. Unfortunately, up to the present time we still lack a thorough examination of the dissolution of the Zurich monasteries and the reappropriation of their assets to education, welfare for the poor, and care for the sick. The following temporary picture can be drawn from the examination of some details:

The Great Minster Foundation was a special case, because it was not totally dissolved; instead, it was maintained as an independent economic and legal entity. This alteration had already begun in the fall of 1523.

Except for Abbess Katharina von Zimmern, there was not a single convent member living in the Mary Minster at this time. These circumstances made it easier for the abbess, who was willing to resign, to transfer the foundation and all its property to the city on October 24, 1524. In accordance with her demand, the Council paid her a pension, commensurate to her station, for the rest of her life. Only the Latin school, the office of people's priest — occupied by Engelhart — and one diaconate were maintained.

Zwingli had already castigated mendicant monks early on, and called their poverty hypocrisy. Starting with that, he had demanded the abolition of mendicant orders and support for the truly poor. These two ideas were joined in his program to change the monasteries into hospitals and welfare institutions, and to incorporate their wealth into the welfare fund. Suggestions like these were common to the Reformation in general.

Following the reorganization of the two foundations, the Council appointed a committee on December 1, 1524 to prepare for the dissolution of the monasteries.[11] The first step in this direction was the establishment of a public assistance program on January 15, 1525 — with the participation of Zwingli — which was intended to eliminate

the practice of begging altogether.[12] The government required the
needy to wear an emblem that gave them the right to take part in
public food programs and in health care. Besides the hospital, it was
the special duty of the Dominican sisters in Oetenbach to care for the
sick. In the summer of the same year, any nuns in the Selnau convent
who were unwilling to leave the order were transferred to the Oetenbach convent, and the convent property was transferred to the
hospital.

A specially created Council committee administered the welfare
fund and was accountable to the Council. In order to build up this
fund, more and more church revenues were transferred to it after
1525, primarily revenues from prebends after the prebendaries had
moved away or died. Out of the thirty-two chapel prebends at the
Great Minster, twenty-three landed in the almoner's office in this
way. The proceeds from fraternities and convents were used next. The
three mendicant monasteries stopped functioning as spiritual institutions; those monks hostile to the Reformation were moved into a
single monastery, where they could live out their last days. The monastery property, with its yearly revenues, came under the administration of a Council caretaker.

In this way the Council secularized church property. However,
they succeeded in doing this only in the city of Zurich, because
patronage rights in the country only belonged to Zurich city institutions or persons in rare cases, and to intervene would have led to
innumerable legal battles with outsiders.

The money was used solely for welfare, in accordance with Zwingli's ideas—but only in the beginning. Monastery property was soon
used for purely secular purposes, such as the defrayal of expenses for
meetings.

3. Reform of the Great Minster

a) *Economic Reorganization*

Acting on Zwingli's maxim that there is no such thing as spiritual
jurisdiction, the foundation itself had petitioned the Council in September 1523 to guarantee its rights. As spiritual authority, the foundation had until then frequently acted in opposition to civil

authority; now it acknowledged explicitly the sovereignty of secular agencies in all questions of law. The Council welcomed this step and signed a contract with the foundation on September 29, 1523, in which relations were regulated.[13]

First of all, the survival of the Great Minster as an economic entity within the Zurich community was assured, and all its rights to the tithe affirmed. On the basis of this economic foundation, the Great Minster was to take care of its new task as a Zurich educational institution, because the Council desired an improvement in Latin studies and theological education. This could only be accomplished very slowly, however, since opposing chaplains and canons had been allowed to keep their prebends. Only after their resignation or death could their vacated positions be used to pay teachers and pastors. In addition, the number of prebends for chaplains and canons were reduced by one-half, and the revenue thus saved was used to establish a scholarship fund and to support the poor.

On August 1, 1523, Zwingli published his *Little Textbook (Lehrbüchlein)*[14] in connection with the foundation's new purpose, in which he stated pedagogical principles in programmatic fashion in accordance with the humanist ideal of education.

b) The Prophecy

No practical steps were undertaken until the spring of 1525. After the death of Canon Johann Niessli on April 3, 1525, who had been hostile to the Reformation and who had administered the Latin school, Zwingli was elected to this post and accorded extensive jurisdiction which entailed, among other things, his move into the official living quarters of the school principal.

Zwingli very quickly succeeded in obtaining from the Council the establishment of a supervisory agency for the whole Zurich school system; he also reorganized the Latin school curriculum at the Great Minster, and saw to it that Jacob Ceporin was hired that same month as teacher of Hebrew and Greek. Ceporin was paid from the vacated prebend of Konrad Hofmann. Following Ceporin's early death, the teaching position was reorganized in January 1527, and one canon's prebend was used for each separate teaching post of Hebrew, Greek, and Latin. It was possible to obtain Konrad Pellikan (1478–1556), born in Alsace, an excellent scholar and a former Franciscan, for the Hebraic studies. He had made a name for himself as the writer of a Hebrew grammar and as a colleague of Erasmus.

By reorganizing the curriculum of the Latin school, Zwingli was able to institutionalize Bible exegesis, which had been carried on only incidentally and cursorily heretofore in Zurich. A few reports indicate that, after the summer of 1520, Zwingli and others had conducted exegetical exercises in private circles in addition to their public serial preaching. Zwingli had dealt with Psalms in 1520.[15] Myconius, the schoolmaster at the Mary Minster, had been doing New Testament exegesis daily since 1524. The "Christian Reputation" of September 1523 had already planned Bible interpretations to be available to everyone. This plan was realized in June 1525, when exegetical lectures open to the public were incorporated into the senior (fourth) grade of the Latin school.

This Bible school received the name "Prophecy" in connection to 1 Cor. 14:26–33.[16] Unfortunately, we lack a thorough investigation of its work as well as of its predecessors and related institutions. This much is clear: according to its position in the educational process, the Prophecy was placed between Latin school and university, since it was in no way intended to replace theological studies at foreign universities. No plans to found a university ever existed.

During the first few years of its existence, the Prophecy served to reeducate and retrain the clergy of the city already in office; they were required to attend the lectures. Due to the paucity of sources, there is very little clarity regarding either the content of the lectures or the faculty. That is why the history of the origins and transmission of Zwingli's exegetical works — all of which originated at this Bible school — is one of the most complicated questions in Zwingli research.

The Prophecy was officially opened on June 19, 1525.[17] With the exception of Fridays and Sundays, canons, city clergy, senior students at the Latin school, and foreign guest scholars assembled every morning in the choir of the Great Minster. During Zwingli's lifetime, only the Old Testament was exegeted there. Following an opening prayer,[18] the Hebrew teacher usually began with an analysis of the original text, Zwingli then interpreted the passage in Latin, on the basis of the Septuagint, and this was followed by an address in German by a preacher, usually Jud. This address rendered the scholars' expositions comprehensible to the people.

Parallel to this work on the Old Testament, the New Testament was dealt with under the leadership of Myconius every afternoon in the Mary Minster choir. Only most recently did the thorough essay by Walter E. Meyers make clear that Zwingli also played a regular part in this location after 1526. At least once a week Zwingli exegeted New Testament texts in Latin at the Mary Minster before the same scholarly audience as at the Great Minster. Following his lecture, he preached at the Vesper service of the Mary Minster.

It can therefore be said, in essence, that Zwingli's exegetical work is characterized by the close correlation of scholarly exegesis and easy-to-understand preaching; that it had its institutional location at the two improved foundation schools of the city; and that it encompassed Old and New Testament series side by side.

c) Zwingli's Exegetical Works

The content of Zwingli's scholarly interpretations and vernacular sermons can be only partially reconstructed. With regard to statements from the pulpit, only a few individual reports about Zwingli's preaching exist at all, and the transmission of his exegetical works is equally burdened by several uncertainties. According to Oskar Farner's[19] and Meyer's[20] reconstructions of Zwingli's interpretations and commentaries or translations of the Old Testament after June 19, 1525, the following have been preserved: Genesis, Exodus, Psalms, Job, Isaiah, Jeremiah, Ezechiel, and the Minor Prophets.[21] Nothing has been preserved of the exegetical work between 1526 and September 1527 on the other books of the Pentateuch or on Joshua, Judges, Ruth, Samuel, and Kings. All the Mary Minster interpretations since 1526 have been preserved: 1 John, 1 and 2 Thessalonians, Colossians, Philippians, Hebrews, 1 and 2 Corinthians, Romans, Mark, John, Matthew, James, and Luke. Zwingli had already dealt with practically the whole New Testament once before in sermons from the Great Minster pulpit.

Zwingli arranged the publication of only Isaiah and Jeremiah out of all the preserved handwritten or printed exegeses; the majority of the other Old Testament exegeses appeared during his lifetime but were based on student notes rather than on his own manuscripts. The editors of these exegeses, especially Jud and Kaspar Megander, obviously did not always distinguish carefully between Zwingli's scholarly exegesis and his popular sermons when copying excerpts. Therefore the commentaries contain sections of Zwingli sermons and even passages from his other published writings. Due to the Prophecy's tendency toward teamwork, it can be assumed that other interpreters' thoughts and expressions were also woven into these exegetical works published under Zwingli's name.

Jud published Zwingli's New Testament exegeses in 1539, but handwritten notes have also been preserved. The detailed relationship between these diverse versions has not yet been investigated. It is to be hoped that the critical edition of Zwingli's works will provide clarity. Until then, there will be great uncertainty about Zwingli's New Testament exegesis.

d) The Zurich Bible

The "Zurich Bible" bears the mark of teamwork even more than the commentaries. Luther's 1522 translation of the New Testament, the *September Testament*, had already been printed in Basel three months after the Wittenberg first printing. However, the Basel edition contained a list of Luther expressions unfamiliar to the Upper Germans and the Swiss, and included appropriate explanations. Two editions of Luther's New Testament, which appeared in Zurich in 1524, went one step further: an unknown editor — occasionally thought to have been Zwingli — adapted Luther's text to native language peculiarities.

A translation of the Old Testament appeared in Wittenberg in individual parts after 1523, and was also reprinted and used in Zurich in revised form between 1525 and 1527. When the translation of the Prophets was too long delayed, Zurich published its own version containing a foreword by Zwingli in 1529.[22] This work originated in the Prophecy. Thus a complete reformatory translation of the Old and New Testaments was available in Zurich by 1529. Additional parts of the Old Testament in the Zurich translation followed, so that the first complete Bible could be printed in Zurich by Christoph Froschauer in 1531; the Old Testament translation of this edition had been thoroughly revised by the Zurich theologians.

No one has as yet attempted to clarify Zwingli's share in this work on the basis of external and stylistic evidence, or by comparing it to his translation in his German writings. Unfortunately, there is an additional lack of a modern edition of either individual parts or the whole of the Zurich Bible.

4. Domestic Relations and Morals Courts

An important step in Zurich's disengagement from episcopal jurisdiction was the settlement of the jurisdictional question regarding the Court of Domestic Relations, which had been a bone of contention between the city and the bishop before the Reformation. A preparatory advisory committee, including both Zwingli and Heinrich Utinger, the episcopal commissioner in the field of Domestic Relations, recommended a new legal procedure for the Domestic Relations court, which became law by its publication on May 10, 1525.[23] Zwingli's part in the composition of the text is not known, which is why he can be considered its author only in a qualified sense. This regulation headed a series of additional ordinances and measures combined in the large mandate of August 23, 1530.[24]

In contrast to existing practice, the new regulations decisively changed marriage laws as well as court jurisdiction. A new agency, completely independent of the bishop, was established. Four secular and three clerical members were appointed to this court of Domestic Relations; the clerics were church lawyer Heinrich Engelhart, People's Priest Jud, and Utinger, the expert episcopal commissioner. Zwingli left the day-to-day work of the Domestic Relations court to others, but he was frequently summoned as witness or expert consultant; Biblical models were drawn upon in establishing legal norms. In contrast to previous laws, obstacles to marriage were drastically reduced, and marriage was prohibited only between blood relatives, in accordance with Lev. 18:6–18. Since marriage was no longer considered a sacrament, and therefore had lost its indissoluble character, it was now possible to terminate marriages through a court decision and thus grant divorces. The primary ground for divorce was adultery, for which divorce and remarriage, after an appropriate waiting period, was expected. Relatively less frequently were marriages dissolved on the grounds of impotence, malicious desertion, or illness.

No case is known of a marriage in Zwingli's time dissolved due to religious differences. A public church ceremony and the registration of the wedding were prescribed for the documentation of a marriage.

In addition, the Court of Domestic Relations had the duty to check the validity of marital promises, to ascertain claims of marriage consummation such as the deflowering of a virgin, and to confirm and judge cases of adultery. One extramarital affair could have far-reaching consequences, since a conviction of adultery carried with it the loss of all offices as well as excommunication. Financial arrangements for weddings and divorces were reserved to the Council.

Since these regulations regulated and supervised a large and important sector of community life, the Court of Domestic Relations expanded its role to encompass that of a court of morals, which was established through a Council ordinance as early as 1526. On March 21, 1526, the judges of the Domestic Relations court were commissioned to take notice of the moral behavior of the citizens.[25] Supervisors of morals, called "marriage counselors" (*Ehegaumer*), were also appointed in rural Zurich. They were supposed to consult, after every worship service, with the appropriate subguardian and the two elders of the parish about the ecclesiastical and moral life of the congregation.

The Zurich Court of Domestic Relations attained superregional significance during its first few years of existence, since it also judged cases from abroad and thus underlined the fact that, for a majority of cases in the Constance diocese, it had substituted for the episcopal court. Other Reformed states of the Confederation later followed Zurich's example: St. Gallen in 1526, Bern in 1528, Basel in 1529, Schaffhausen in 1529, Glarus in 1530; also, in Southern Germany, Constance in 1531, Ulm in 1531, Esslingen in 1532, Strasbourg in 1530, and others. The newly created Courts of Domestic Relations maintained good relations with each other with regard to preachers in particular, and tried to standardize their verdicts, which they succeeded in doing for the most part. But on the other hand, there were extensive disagreements among them on the closely related issue of church discipline.

Zwingli wavered for a long time on the issue of whether it was the congregation or the civil government which had the right to impose disciplinary measures such as exclusion from the Lord's Supper (*excommunicatio minor*) or total excommunication (*excommunicatio maior*). As late as 1525, Zwingli was still allocating the authority to excommunicate to the congregation,[26] but the Zurich Council rejected such relative autonomy on the part of any spiritual authority.[27] Zwingli himself recognized the practical impossibility of setting up a purely ecclesiastical agency under the circumstances existing in Zurich, where the ties between spiritual and secular authority were close. Moreover, the Court of Domestic Relations provided a perfect example of functioning teamwork between the two powers.

Zwingli increasingly defended the magistrate's right to impose the ban. However, he added the proviso that the culprit should first have been warned by the "congregation," that is, by its representatives such as pastor, guild master, marriage counselor, or subguardian. Thus the ban was handled in a two-step process, with the Council having the right to make the final decision.

There were objections to this model. In Basel, John Oecolampadius raised serious objections to it during Zwingli's lifetime, saying that the congregation, not the government, should have the responsibility of imposing the ban. Zwingli was unable to convince Oecolampadius, and so church discipline was exercised in a variety of ways in German Switzerland. Unfortunately, no comparative investigation has yet been carried out which would reveal the distinguishing features of Zwingli's understanding of church discipline.

5. Worship Service, Ecclesiastical Art, Zwingli's Songs

Although the Council acceded to the wishes of Zwingli and his friends with regard to the issue of images, and allowed the churches to be cleared of them in June 1524, it hesitated to abolish the mass and did not accept Zwingli's suggestion to hold a daily morning sermon followed by communion instead of a morning mass.[28] On the other hand, after the rapid decrease in traditional exercises of piety during the winter of 1523–24, the Council no longer made any effort to enforce previous mass practices as binding without exception. Pastors were actually released from the duty of celebrating mass and could alter the rubrics as they thought fit.

This confused and disorganized situation prompted Zwingli to design a communion liturgy in the German language, *Act or Custom of the Supper (Aktion oder Brauch des Nachtmahls)*.[29] Shortly before Easter 1525, he and his most intimate friends (Engelhart, Jud, Myconius, Megander) went before the Council to request the cancellation of the mass and the introduction of a new public order of worship. The Council acceded to this request surprisingly quickly, on Wednesday of Holy Week. The timing was in no way coincidental, for a communion service in accord with Zwingli's theological ideas could then be celebrated for the first time on the following day — Maundy Thursday, the day commemorating Jesus' last meal.

The framework and proceedings of the worship service were characterized by clarity and simplicity: organ music and singing disappeared. In order to avoid outward display, the metal eucharistic implements were replaced by wooden patens and cups. The congregation sat at set tables to emphasize the meal aspect. However, the sermon was the focal point of the worship service, and this was underlined not only by the liturgical rubrics but also by Zwingli's proposal to limit the celebration of communion to four times a year, namely, Christmas, Easter, Pentecost, and "Autumn." There is some doubt as to whether that meant the feast day of the Great Minster patron saints Felix and Regula, on September 11,[30] or All Saints Day, November 1.[31] Moreover, it appears that in actual practice communion was celebrated only three times a year. In any case, Zwingli limited the use of the sacrament of the altar as no other reformer did, although it must be noted that this does not represent a great departure from late medieval communion practices.

Only the proceedings of the communion service are described in the liturgical outline of *Act or Custom of the Supper*. In contrast to the Lutheran rubrics, the traditional Canon of the Mass has almost disappeared in this version. Zwingli did not have to describe the procedure for the preceding service of the word because he followed the rubrics of the pre-Reformation Service of the Word as it had been carried out, for example, by the people holding preaching posts.

Jud's booklet on baptism of 1523 contained a new order of baptism. It was further revised by Zwingli in May 1525, in his book *On Baptism, Anabaptism, and Infant Baptism (Von der Taufe, von der Wiedertaufe und von der Kindertaufe)*.[32] It took into account Zwingli's anticatholic as well as his antianabaptist orientation and also expressed his sacramental theology clearly.

Zurich's regulations regarding public worship were combined before Zwingli's death in the undated *Regulation of the Christian Church in Zurich (Ordnung der christlichen Kirche zu Zurich)*,[33] which was probably done in 1528 or 1529[34] and did not make any basic changes from the regulations of 1525. There is, however, some question as to whether and to what extent actual worship practices in Zurich and other states really followed the published orders, since source documents regarding worship proceedings at the time of Zwingli lead to the conclusion that there were many differences. This problem was most clearly recognized by Marcus Jenny, who best illuminated Zurich's liturgical practices by drawing upon parallel documents from other cities.

Zwingli denied any religious usefulness whatever to pictorial representations, and enlarged upon that in greatest detail in his *A Response Given to Valentin Compar (Eine Antwort, Valentin Compar gegeben)*.[35] He thought that the danger of paintings or statues leading to cultic veneration was much greater than any possible usefulness they could have as a "Bible for illiterate people" (*Biblia pauperum*). He declared that one should give the money directly to the poor rather than buying and donating images.

Because of his rejection on principle, statues of saints and altar paintings were removed from Zurich churches and murals were painted over; all the plain Christian symbols, like crosses, also disappeared.

Zwingli frequently made pejorative comments about church music, aimed particularly at priestly chanting and monastic choirs. As Markus Jenny stressed, this criticism dates from the year 1523, when Zwingli most sharply attacked the practices of the traditional church. Zwingli brought up music in connection with images and vestments, which, like all other medieval pious exercises, could divert people from the sole true, inner, spiritual worship service. What Zwingli thought about the early Protestant church musical practices, for instance in Lutheranism, is not known. Nor did he ever express himself on congregational singing in Zurich. He did approve of simple chanting, a recitation sung on a single set note. Perhaps his opposition on principle to liturgical music cannot be proven, but on the other hand Zwingli made no effort to encourage congregational singing, for instance, singing Psalms, with which he was familiar from his stay in Strasbourg.

Three songs under Zwingli's name have been preserved: "Plague Song" (*Pestlied*), (Help, Lord God, Help);[36] the "Kappel Song" (*Kappelerlied*), (Lord, now lift the wagon yourself); and a revision of Psalm 69 (Help, God, the Water). Although Jenny dealt with them extensively, not all questions of authorship and date of composition have been resolved completely.

In any case, one certainty is that these were not songs to be sung at worship services, but rather solos in the "house music" style of his day.[37] Therefore they should in no way be identified with hymns of the Reformation, even though they found their way into song reprints and hymnals in the sixteenth century. Only the "Kappel Song" succeeded as a hymn. Zwingli probably composed the melody for the "Plague Song" and "Kappel Song" himself.

6. Bibliography

Reformatory Movement and Social Situation

Hauswirth, Rene. "Die Zürcher Obristmeister (Oberstzunftmeister), 1518–1547." *Zwingliana* 12 (1967): 596–602.

Jacob, Walter. *Politische Führungsschichte und Reformation. Untersuchungen zur Reformation in Zürich 1519–1528*. Zürcher Beiträge zur Reformationsgeschichte 1. Zurich, 1970.

Muralt, Leonhard von. "Zum Problem der Theokratie bei Zwingli." In *Discordia Concors. Festschrift für Edgar Bonjour*, 2: 367–90. Basel and Stuttgart, 1968.

Ramp, Ernst. *Das Zinsproblem. Eine historische Untersuchung*. Quellen und Abhandlungen zur Geschichte des schweizerischen Protestantismus 4. Zurich, 1949.

Rich, Arthur. "Zwingli als sozialpolitischer Denker." *Zwingliana* 13 (1969): 67–89.

Schelbert, Leo. "Jacob Grebel's Trial Revised." *Archiv für Reformationsgeschichte* 60 (1969): 32–64.

Stayer, James M. "Die Anfänge des schweizerischen Täufertums im reformierten Kongregationalismus. In Hans-Jürgen Goertz, ed, *Umstrittenes Täufertum, 1525–1975. Neue Forschungen*, 19–49. 2d ed. Göttingen, 1977.

Dissolution of Monasteries and Welfare Measures;
Reform of the Great Minster

Büsser, Fritz. "Théorie et pratique de l'éducation sous la Réforme à Zurich." In Jean Boisset, ed., *La Réforme et l'éducation*, 153–69. Toulouse, 1974.

Figi, Jacques. *Die innere Reorganisation des Grossmünsterstiftes in Zürich von 1519 bis 1531.* Zürcher Beiträge zur Geschichtswissenschaft 9. Zurich, 1951.

Gut, Walter. "Zwingli als Erzieher." *Zwingliana* 6 (1936): 289–306.

Köhler, Walther. "Armenpflege und Wohltätigkeit in Zürich zur Zeit Ulrich Zwinglis. Zürich 1919." In *119th Neujahrsblatt.* Published by Hülfsgesellschaft in Zurich in 1919.

Künzli, Edwin. "Zwingli als Ausleger des Alten Testaments." In *Huldrych Zwingli sämtliche Werke*, ed. Emil Egli et al., XIV:860–89.

———. "Quellenproblem und mystischer Schriftsinn in Zwinglis Genesis- und Exoduskommentar." *Zwingliana* 9 (1950): 185–207; 9 (1951): 253–307.

Meyer, Walter. "Die Entstehung von Huldrych Zwinglis neutestamentlichen Kommentaren und Predigtnachschriften." *Zwingliana* 13 (1976): 285–331.

Mezger, J. J. *Geschichte der deutschen Bibelübersetzungen in der schweizerisch-reformierten Kirche.* Basel, 1876. Reprint. Nieuwkoop, 1967.

Rüsch, Ernst Gerhard. "Die Erziehungsgrundsätze Huldrych Zwinglis." In *Vom Heiligen in der Welt. Beiträge zur Kirchen- und Geistesgeschichte*, 72–98. Zollikon, 1959.

———. "Die humanistischen Vorbilder der Erziehungsschrift Zwinglis." *Theologische Zeitschrift* 22 (1966): 122–47.

Schweizer, Paul. "Die Behandlung der zürcherischen Klostergüter in der Reformationszeit." *Theologische Zeitschrift aus der Schweiz* 2 (1885): 161–88.

Spillmann, Kurt. "Zwingli und die Zürcher Schulverhältnisse." *Zwingliana* 11 (1962): 427–48.

Steinmann, Ruth. *Die Benediktinerinnenabtei zum Fraumünster und ihr Verhältnis zur Stadt Zürich 853–1524.* Studien und Mitteilungen zur Geschichte des Benediktiner-Ordens und seiner Zweige. Ergänzungsband 23. St. Ottilien, 1980.

Zimmerli-Witschi, Alice. *Frauen in der Reformationszeit.* Zurich, 1981. Information about Katharina von Zimmern is on pp. 15–18.

Zürcher, Christoph. *Pellikans Wirken in Zurich, 1526–1556.* Zürcher Beiträge zur Reformationsgeschichte 4. Zurich, 1975.

Domestic Relations and Morals Courts

Kilchenmann, Küngolt. "Die Organisation des zürcherischen Ehegerichts zur Zeit Zwinglis. Rechts- und staatswissenschaftliche. Ph.D. diss., Zürich, 1946.

Köhler, Walther. "Zwingli vor Ehegericht." In *Festgabe des Zwingli-Vereins zum 70. Geburtstag seines Präsidenten Hermann Escher*, 166–69. Zurich, 1927.

————. *Zürcher Ehegericht und Genfer Konsistorium.* Vol. 1, *Das Zürcher Ehegericht und seine Auswirkung in der deutschen Schweiz zur Zeit Zwinglis.* Quellen und Abhandlungen zur Schweizerischen Reformationsgeschichte 7. Leipzig, 1932.

Ley, Roger. *Kirchenzucht bei Zwingli.* Quellen und Abhandlungen zur Geschichte des schweizerischen Protestantismus 2. Zurich 1948.

Worship Service, Ecclesiastical Art, Zwingli's Songs

Campenhausen, Hans Freiherr von. "Die Bilderfrage in der Reformation." In *Traditionen und Leben. Kräfte der Kirchengeschichte. Aufsätze und Vorträge*, 361–407. Tübingen, 1960.

————. *Tradition and Life in the Church. Essays and Lectures in Church History.* Translated by A. V. Littledale. Philadelphia, 1968.

Garside, Charles. *Zwingli and the Arts.* 2d ed. Yale Historical Publications 33. New Haven and London, 1982.

Jenny, Markus. *Zwinglis Stellung zur Musik im Gottesdienst.* Schriftenreihe des Arbeitskreises für evangelische Kirchenmusik 3. Zurich, 1966.

————. *Die Einheit des Abendmahlsgottesdienstes bei den elsässischen und schweizerischen Reformatoren.* Studien zur Dogmengeschichte und systematischen Theologie 23. Zurich and Stuttgart, 1968.

————. "Die Lieder Zwinglis." *Jahrbuch für Liturgik und Hymnologie* 14 (1969): 63–102 (with reprints).

————. "Geschichte und Verbreitung der Lieder Zwinglis." In *Kerygma und Melos. Christhard Mahrenholz 70 Jahre, 11. August 1970*, 319–41. Kassel, Basel, Tours, London, Berlin, and Hamburg, 1970.

Old, Hughes Oliphant. *The Patristic Roots of Reformed Worship.* Zürcher Beiträge zur Reformationsgeschichte 5. Zurich, 1975.

Schmidt-Clausing, Fritz. *Zwingli als Liturgiker. Eine liturgiegeschichtliche Untersuchung.* Veröffentlichungen der Evangelischen Gesellschaft für Liturgieforschung 7. Göttingen, 1952.

————. "Die Neudatierung der liturgischen Schriften Zwinglis." *Theologische Zeitschrift* 25 (1969): 252–65.

————, ed. *Zwinglis liturgische Formulare.* Frankfurt am Main, 1970.

————. "Die liturgietheologische Arbeit Zwinglis am Sintflutgebet des Taufformulars. Ein weiterer Blick in Zwinglis liturgische Werkstatt." *Zwingliana* 13 (1972): 516–43; 13 (1973): 591–615.

Schweizer, Julius. *Reformierte Abendmahlsgestaltung in der Schau Zwinglis.* Basel, 1954.

VII

REFORMATION IN THE CONFEDERATION (1524–1529)

1. The Baden Disputation of 1526

After April 8, 1524, when Lucerne, Uri, Schwyz, Unterwalden, and Zug entered into an alliance (joined by Freiburg and Solothurn a little later) these Five States headed the Catholic defense against Zwingli's Reformation. They made contact with Luther's opponents in the empire through Suffragan Bishop John Fabri. They planned to prosecute Zwingli as an adherent of the Wittenberg reformer and place him under the imperial ban. Still in 1524, John Eck, the professor of theology at Ingolstadt who had debated Luther in 1519 in Leipzig, offered to dispute with Zwingli. This suggestion agreed with Zwingli's own intentions, which is why he, like the Confederates, approved such a plan.[1]

But once again the conflict, as in the Zurich disputation, was over the appropriate judging authority. Zwingli insisted on Scripture as norm, declaring that only Scripture is the judge of all human beings.[2] Eck, on the other hand, demanded a board of experts, for books spoke only through skilled judges.[3] This argument was soon pushed into the background by the peasant uprising that preoccupied both Protestants and Catholics.

In the fall of 1525, Eck resumed his plan by making formal petition to the Confederation. Although Zwingli and the Zurich Council basically agreed to Zwingli's participation in the disputation, they nevertheless rejected as unacceptable the procedural conditions proposed. They asserted that because of its Catholic majority Baden was an unsuitable location for the debate; that Bern, Constance, or some other place would be preferable; and that the promise of safe conduct could not be relied upon, in view of the executions of Zwingli adherents. Above all, Zwingli denied that the Diet was competent to function as a court and make judgments in matters of faith. His objections were based on his realistic assessment of the number of votes favoring him on this board. Zurich could not hope to draw a majority of the undecided states to its side against the Five States.

By furthermore refusing to view the Worms decisions as applicable to the Confederation, Zwingli introduced a "national" element. If he had earlier accused Catholics of deserting the practices and tradition of the fathers, he now charged them with restricting the liberty of the Swiss,[4] since they were acknowledging the authority of the German Diet. Zwingli's counterdemands, which Zurich adopted as its official preconditions, were based on the concept of letting individual states decide the question of Reformation. Thus these conditions aimed at the disputation's failure as a meeting of the Confederation as a whole.

The disputation took place despite Zwingli's boycott. The meeting in Baden began on May 19, 1526. All the Confederates had sent delegates, although Zurich's representatives did not participate in the sessions. The Catholic party was led by Eck, the Protestant party by John Oecolampadius from Basel. For four weeks the disputation concerned itself with seven main theses presented by the Ingoldstadt professor, who expertly pointed out differences of opinion within the anti-Catholic camp, between for instance, Zwingli and Luther. His intention was to demonstrate the uselessness of the Bible — to which, after all, all Protestants appealed — as authority.

Zwingli, twenty-five kilometers away in Baden, was being kept accurately informed of the proceedings, so that he was able to make his opinions known in quickly printed pamphlets: *The First Short Response to Eck's Seven Concluding Statements (Die erste kurze Antwort über Ecks sieben Schlussreden)* on May 21, 1526; and *The Other Response to Several Untrue Responses that Eck Gave in Baden (Die andere Antwort über etliche unwahrhafte Antworten die Eck zu Baden Gegeben)* on June 3, 1526.[5] In these pamphlets, "Swiss distrust of foreigners is strongly fanned,"[6] but Zwingli's statements found no echo.

Zwingli's teaching was condemned as heretical in the decision of

June 9, 1526. The juridical consequences of this decision were drawn in occasionally direct quotations from the verdict against Luther: Zwingli should be considered banned, and the dissemination of his writings was prohibited. In conclusion, the Diet specifically endorsed the teaching office of the church in interpreting Scripture, and established existing worship practices as untouchable.

These results were by no means based on a unanimous vote of the thirteen Confederates. The Zurich Reformation was condemned by Glarus, Solothurn, Freiburg, and Appenzell in addition to the Five States. In opposition were Bern, Basel, Schaffhausen, and of course Zurich.

The Baden disputation failed to achieve its goal, since the undecided parties were driven into the arms of Zurich by the Catholic winners' gloating statements over those powers willing to reform. Although one had hoped to obtain a general Confederation condemnation of Zwingli and his followers by this undertaking, this disputation proved that a deep rift existed in the federation on the issue of religion. Precisely what had been considered Confederational was now in doubt.

2. Confessional Division of
the Confederation
(1526–1529)

During the years immediately following the Baden disputation, the antagonism between the religious factions increased to the point of open war. This development led to the confessional division of the country. The following points are characteristic of this period:

1. Social and economic contrasts between rural and urban territories were further heightened by religious tensions.

2. In accordance with Zwingli's concept of Reformation, the Protestants strongly attacked the alleged moral corruption of the rural states—namely, the enlistment of mercenaries and the pension system—as well as the traditional piety of the Catholics. These attacks struck a vital nerve in these communities.

3. If there had been only occasional contact with foreign sympathizers previously, from now on both confessional parties entered into formal alliances with non-Confederation partners.

4. The political and constitutional presuppositions of the Con-

federation and its system of alliances and dialogues were increasingly being questioned. The Protestant side, due to its ranking of scriptural authority above Confederation tradition, tended to drop previous normal practices.

5. Zwingli influenced this development in three ways: first, he supported the reformatory movement outside Zurich with his presence; second, he expressed his opinion of existing decisions either in print or in letters; third, he contributed to Zurich's formation of political will by his increased participation in various commissions.

These decisions determined Zurich's behavior on the Confederation level. Because of the territorial and juridical breakup of the Confederation, this development leading to confessionalization was composed of a chaotic number of disparate elements. The following must be singled out in connection with Zwingli's achievements.

The city of St. Gallen, as an Affiliated State, had a particular relationship to the Confederation. Its Reformation history had been determined by its mayor, the scholar Joachim Vadian, who had had connections with Zwingli since at least the start of Zwingli's time in Glarus. St. Gallen abolished the mass two years after Zurich, which made it the first city in the Confederation to follow Zurich in introducing the Reformation. The late 1520s were marked by quarrels between the city and the abbey of St. Gallen.

No other state of the Confederation imitated Zurich as closely as did neighboring Schaffhausen. Its Reformation history resembled that of Zurich, for example, in early humanist currents in the All Saints monastery, or in a parallel constellation in the relation of the Large to the Small Council. Here too the governing board of the Large Council demonstrated greater approval of the Reformation. Zwingli's ideas had been disseminated since 1522 by Sebastian Hofmeister, a Franciscan monk who had presided at the first Zurich disputation in 1523.

Schaffhausen was the only Confederate state that experienced a split within the reformatory party into a Zwinglian and a Lutheran faction during Zwingli's lifetime. Only in 1536 could the conflict be resolved by dismissing both leaders, Erasmus Ritter and Benedict Burgauer. Zwingli intervened in the conflict several times in favor of Ritter,[7] and encouraged his protégé by letters.

Schaffhausen took Zurich's side in the argument about the Baden disputation; but it took the Large Council until 1529 to freeze out the Small Council, an action that allowed the official introduction of the Reformation in September 1529. Both decisions were made in the presence of Zurich delegates, who had applied pressure on their small northern neighbor.

Zwingli was connected to no other foreign theologian as intimately as to Oecolampadius, the Basel theologian who came from Württemberg.[8] Zwingli carried on an extensive and friendly correspondence with him. As Zwingli's substitute, Oecolampadius had also defended the Zurich preacher at the Baden disputation. According to Walther Köhler's feasible judgment, Zwingli's importance in Basel grew in proportion to Erasmus's withdrawal.[9]

The Catholic Confederates considered Basel to have been in Zurich's camp since 1524; actually the issue of the Reformation in Basel had not yet been resolved at that time. The Basel government did not in any way sanction the reformatory changes in the early years with official decrees. From 1525 until 1529, both the celebration of the mass and Protestant communion services existed side by side. The reversal was brought about by a popular uprising under the leadership of the guilds. The riots ended in a storming of the churches and the destruction of images on February 9, 1529, and the resignation of the traditionalist councilmen. The mass was prohibited in city and rural areas; an April 1, 1529 church order followed the Zurich model.

Unpleasant experiences with the Basel government left Oecolampadius skeptical about its authority in church matters, which contributed to his fundamental difference with Zwingli on the issue of church discipline.

3. Reformation in Bern

Bern's political situation differed in many respects from that of Zurich. The city/state was governed by an aristocratic elite who earned large revenues from the pension system. Bern did not experience a guild revolution like Zurich, which is why the guilds there had no political significance at the beginning of the sixteenth century. Foreign policy was affected by its relationship to Savoy, its restless neighbor to the southwest. Bern was extremely interested in peace with France and in a united Confederation in order to be able to hold these threatening forces in check. That is why Zurich's expansionary Reformation policies in the north and east of the Confederation were received coolly in Bern. On the whole, the policy of this city on the Aar revealed clearly conservative traits.

As in Zurich and Schaffhausen, the most important reformatory impulses in Bern emanated from the leading religious foundations in the city. Unfortunately, we still do not have a comparative examination of the role played by the minsters, foundations, and monasteries as seedbeds of reformatory preaching in the Confederation. Nor is sufficient attention being paid to the fact that all the trend-setting preachers were outsiders. A study from the viewpoint of social history about the clergy could yield valuable insights.

Berchtold Haller, born in the region of Rottweil, had presided as people's priest since 1519 at the St. Vincent Minster in Bern, where Nicholas von Waltenwyl was a canon and, since 1523, abbot. His personal encounter with Zwingli had already strengthened the bond between the two people's priests in the early 1520s. Just as in Basel, the city Council refused to support the church-critical movement formally, but did allow the "preaching of the gospel" as early as 1522, without abolishing celibacy, fasting practices, and veneration of saints. On the contrary, preserving these customs was still being specially mandated in 1524.

An extensive propaganda campaign attempted to influence public opinion in Bern. Nicholas Manuel (1484–1530), the poet, painter, and politician, most clearly expressed the morally corrupting influence of the mercenary and pension systems in his plays, which, in total agreement with Zwingli's opinions, blamed the pope for these conditions.

Just before the Baden disputation, Bern was still straddling the fence between Zurich and the Five States, and prohibited the marriage of priests during the negotiations. Nevertheless, the aftereffects of the debate brought about a reversal: Bern broke with the Catholic party and the reformatory party chalked up some gains in Bern itself. Haller, for example, was released from his duty to celebrate mass.

The breakthrough came with the Council election at Easter 1527, when — possibly due to impressions of an impending economic crisis — a majority of councilmen desiring reform were installed in the Large Council. Unfortunately, we do not have a detailed investigation of this transfer of political and social power in Bern. In any case, it seems certain that here, as in Basel and Zurich, it was initiated by the guilds, which were able to win over the conservative powers concentrated especially in the rural area.

In order to achieve both domestic and external clarity once and for all, the city government decided to use the method, by now used several times, of holding a disputation; from the very beginning its intention was to supersede the Baden disputation. Thus the plan of an inter-Confederational assembly serving the Reformation, which Zwingli had developed in 1523 against Niklaus von Wattenwyl, was realized after all.

Besides the Bern clergy, participants in the disputation included a strong Zurich delegation led by Zwingli, pastors from other Protestant states of the Confederation and imperial cities of Upper Germany — like Martin Bucer and Wolfgang Capito from Strasbourg, Ambrose Blarer from Constance, and Andreas Althamer from Nürnberg. The total was about three hundred and fifty Bern pastors and one hundred outsiders. The meeting lasted almost three weeks, from January 6–26. 1528. When the Catholic states, as well as the theologians Eck and Fabri, refused to attend, the Catholic side was sparsely represented. Konrad Treger, the Augustinian Provincial from Freiburg, who was their most important speaker, had already walked out in anger and returned home on the fifth day.

The disputation was under Zwingli's spell with regard to theology. The man from Zurich had already reviewed, and probably corrected,[10] the ten disputation theses drafted by Bern preachers.[11] It is not clear exactly who wrote the theses, but they were derived from earlier disputations and particularly from Zwingli's writings, and some of them directly refuted statements Eck had made in Baden. Their form and content were in accord with Zwingli's convictions. Zwingli had also given advice on arrangements to Haller, who in turn made suggestions to the Council.

There are reliable reports on the proceedings of the debate.[12] Zwingli took the floor more than one hundred times[13] and shared the main burden of defending the Reformation position with Haller and Franz

Kolb of Bern and with Oecolampadius, Bucer, and Capito. Once again the debate centered on the usual themes: concept of church, authority of Scripture, the mass, veneration of saints, images, and marriage of priests. But the intra-Protestant conflicts over communion also surfaced when Benedict Burgauer and Andreas Althamer defended the Lutheran view.

The disputation provided the proof of the legitimacy of Protestant teaching and practice that the government had desired. The consequences were drawn at once: on January 27, the Council ordered the abolition of the mass and of images; on February 2, it required all the citizens in the city to take an oath to obey future ordinances, which represents a first in the history of the Reformation. A decree dated February 7, 1528 established the Reformation in both city and country.

Zwingli himself had delivered a blueprint for this edict,[14] which was followed extensively. Since this Reformation decree had cleared the way for an orderly Protestant ecclesiastical system in Bern, Zwingli was called "founder of Bern's Reformed Church."[15]

During his stay in Bern, Zwingli preached twice in the minster, on January 19 and 30, 1528. These sermons were quickly published, although the second text represents only an abridged version.[16]

The *First Sermon*[17] exegeted the Apostles' Creed in order to establish agreement between the preacher and all true believers. It is one in a series of other sermons and treatises in which Zwingli intended to "give an account of his faith"[18] in concentrated form. The structure of the sermon is typical of Zwingli's thought process: starting with God's attributes ("the supreme and true Good")[19] he designated every iota of trust in the creaturely worthless; in his wisdom, God rules the world by the power of predetermination and prevenience (*fürordnung und fürsichtigkeyt*),[20] which humankind insufficiently recognizes, to its cost. It is in the salvation of a human being in God's only Son Jesus Christ that these qualities are taught.[21] This argumentation confirms Zwingli's principle that only trust in the divine can give a human being salvation and certainty. Zwingli spoke so extensively about Jesus' ascension while dealing with the text of the Creed,[22] that other parts of the Creed could only be treated sparingly. Zwingli's theological concern during these years was marked by the weight he assigned to his doctrine of God and to his view of the Lord's Supper. With regard to the latter, his understanding of sacrament can be viewed as the application of his basic insight of God's spiritual essence.

The *Second Sermon*,[23] preached on the day before his departure, deals with the steadfastness of the Christian.

The disputation brought Bern a Reformation order on the Zurich model, up to and including the establishment of a school modeled after the Prophecy. With regard to economically significant changes, however, progress was more hesitant. Enlistment of mercenaries and receiving pensions were not prohibited until 1530.

On the whole, Bern experienced as extensive an interpenetration of ecclesiastical and civic powers as anywhere else in the Confederation. It is true that Zurich was also heading in this direction, but after the catastrophic defeat in Kappel in 1531—which set off a crisis of confidence between politicians and the clergy—it was implemented very reluctantly. In the Confederation view, the Bern disputation ended Zurich's isolation and simultaneously established the virtual split of the Confederation into two religious parties.

4. Confessional Alliances and Common Lordships (First Kappel War)

The results of the Bern disputation speeded up several cities' conversion to the Reformation and institutionalized their mutual ties by way of formal covenantal responsibilities. As early as December 1527, Zurich had signed a treaty to defend the Reformation, the so-called Christian Fortress Law, with the city of Constance; in 1528 Bern and St. Gallen joined the alliance, and Basel, Schaffhausen, Biel, and Mülhausen (in Alsace) did so in 1529. These allies strove to coordinate their religious foreign policies, and to provide, through close ties, their domestic preachers with as much uniformity in teaching and practice as possible.

The Five States felt encircled as a result of the disputation, which is why they looked for outside allies. On April 22, 1529, they entered into a "Christian Union" with the Austrian government of King Ferdinand. Thus the confessional opposition between the Five States (along with the two Catholic cities of Freiburg and Solothurn) on the one side and the members of the Christian Fortress Law (including the Protestant cities of Zurich, Bern, St. Gallen, Schaffhausen, Basel, and Biel) on the other side was apparently firmly established by 1529.

This split among the governing states necessarily affected their joint administration of the vassal districts and their perception of joint responsibilities toward the Affiliated States. Each of the two parties tried to succeed in carrying out its own church-political intentions.

With regard to the Common Lordships, it was a question of who would have to make the decision for or against the Reformation. The Christian Fortress Law cities were of the opinion that it was up to a majority decision of the individual congregations to abolish the mass and install reformatory preachers. This view contradicted the understanding of law of the Five States, and so they decided that the respective governing states had to judge the question of religion for the affected Common Lordship as a whole and that the guardian appointed by them had to act accordingly. This attitude is understandable, when one remembers that the Catholic Confederates had the majority vote in the administration of all the larger protectorates and could thus block the Reformation. To the Catholic objection that even in Zurich and Bern the Reformation had been introduced by the government and not the congregation, Zwingli replied that the Christian congregation was formed by the guild communities who were then represented by councils and citizens, and that the will to reform had started in the guilds.[24]

The two parties found themselves in a constitutional stalemate. Tension increased when Catholic Unterwalden fomented peasant uprisings in the upper regions of Bern, and especially when the Reformation movement spread with increasing success in the Independent State of Aargau. It was possible in this way to establish a territorial link between Zurich and Bern which threatened to seal off Interior Switzerland from its extremely important political and economic access to the north.

Soon after the treaty was signed between the Interior states and Austria, the Zurich-born preacher Jacob Kaiser was executed in Schwyz. This humiliation of Zurich made war inevitable. Just as he had already done in 1525–26 in his *Battleplan (Plan zu einem Feld-zug)*,[25] Zwingli, probably with the participation of army officers, drafted some *Advice About the War (Ratschlag über den Krieg)*[26] for the government, stating not only Zurich's justification for an attack on the Catholic states but also suggesting concrete political and military measures to be taken.

But opposition to these war plans was growing in Zurich itself, and especially in Bern; only when Zwingli threatened to resign, on June 9, 1529, could this opposition be broken. (However, this report of Zwingli's threatened resignation cannot be accepted without some doubt.[27]) War was declared.

The armies encountered each other in the vicinity of Kappel. The approximately thirty thousand men on the Bern and Zurich side faced a mere nine thousand Interior Swiss men, who had been abandoned by Austria. The moderate enthusiasm for war on the part of Bern, the inferior number of Interior Swiss, and the effect of a food blockade furthered both parties' willingness to negotiate. Ceding to pressure from its allies, Zurich ignored Zwingli's written goals for war and negotiation and made peace.

Zwingli had demanded the dissolution of the Christian Union; unhindered "preaching of the gospel" in all areas of the Confederation (and thus also in Interior Switzerland and in the Common Lordships); a general prohibition of the pension system; and payment of war reparations to Zurich and Bern.[28] In the First Kappel Peace Treaty of June 26, 1529, the Catholic states pledged only to dissolve their alliance with Ferdinand and to apply the congregation principle in the Common Lordships and Affiliated States. The demand for Protestant preaching in Catholic territories was left unresolved, and any prohibition of pensions was out of the question. Nevertheless, the peace treaty secured the legal basis for the establishment of the Reformation in large parts of north and east Switzerland.

These results embittered Zwingli. Apart from the treaty's lack of clarity with regard to reformatory preaching in Interior Switzerland, he found the thought of the preservation of the pension system unbearable. His plans for the reform of the Confederation had suffered a clear setback. Furthermore, it had become evident that Zurich politicians were unwilling to follow Zwingli's ambitious plans unconditionally. This was the beginning of an estrangement between Zwingli and the political leaders of the city.

5. Bibliography

Bender, Wilhelm. *Zwinglis Reformationsbündnisse. Untersuchungen zur Rechts- und Sozialgeschichte der Burgrechtsverträge eid genössischer und oberdeutscher Städte zur Ausbreitung und Sicherung der Reformation Zwinglis.* Zurich and Stuttgart, 1970.

Guggisberg, Hans Rudolf, and Hans Füglister, "Die Basler Weberzunft als Trägerin reformatorischer Propaganda." In Bernd Moeller, ed., *Stadt und Kirche,* 48–56. Schriften des Vereins für Reformationsgeschichte 190. Gütersloh, 1978.

Haas, Martin. *Zwingli und der Erste Kappelerkrieg.* Zurich, 1965. Abridged in *Zwingliana* 12 (1964): 35–68; 93–136.

Hendricks, Dan L. "The Bern Disputation. Some Observations." *Zwingliana* 14 (1978): 565–75.

Im Hof, Ulrich. "Die Gründung der Hohen Schule zu Bern 1528." *Berner Zeitschrift für Geschichte und Heimatkunde* 40 (1978): 249–59. Also in *450 Jahre Berner Hohe Schule, 1528–1978,* 9–19. Bern, 1978.

Kägi, Ursula. "Die Aufnahme der Reformation in den ostschweizerischen Untertanengebieten – der Weg Zürichs zu einem obrigkeitlichen Kirchenregiment bis zum Frühjar 1529." Ph.D. diss., Zurich, 1972.

Köhler, Walther. "Zwingli und Basel." *Zwingliana* 5 (1929): 2–10.

Lavater, Hans Rudolf. "Regnum Christi etiam externum – Huldrych Zwinglis Brief vom 4. Mai 1528 an Ambrosius Blarer in Konstanz." *Zwingliana* 15 (1981): 338–81.

Locher, Gottfried W. "Die Berner Disputation 1528. Charakter, Verlauf, Bedeutung und theologischer Gehalt." *Zwingliana* 14 (1978): 542–64.

———. "Von der Standhaftigkeit. Zwinglis Schlusspredigt an der Berner Disputation als Beitrag zu seiner Ethik." In Ulrich Neuenschwander and Rudolf Dellsperger, eds., *Humanität und Glaube. Gedenkschrift für Kurt Guggisberg,* 29–41. Bern and Stuttgart, 1973.

Moser, Andres. "Die Anfänge der Freundschaft zwischen Zwingli und Ökolampad." *Zwingliana* 10 (1958): 614–20.

Muralt, Leonhard von. *Die Badener Disputation.* Quellen und Abhandlungen zur Schweizerischen Reformationsgeschichte 3. Leipzig, 1926.

———. "Zwinglis Reformation in der Eidgenossenschaft." *Zwingliana* 13 (1969): 19–33.

Vasella, Oskar. *Österreich und die Bündnispolitik der katholischen Orte 1527–1529.* Feiburger Universitätsreden, Neue Folge 11. Freiburg in der Schweiz, 1951.

Vierhundertfünfzig Jahre Berner Reformation. Beiträge zur Geschichte der Berner Reformation und zu Niklaus Manuel. Historischen Verein des Kantons Bern. Bern, 1980.

Wipf, Jakob. "Zwinglis Beziehungen zu Schaffhausen." *Zwingliana* 5 (1929): 11–41.

VIII
CONFLICT ABOUT THE SACRAMENTS

1. The Argument with Anabaptists

In December 1523, when the Zurich Council once again postponed any changes in the mass — not really running counter to Zwingli's wishes, but nevertheless without his explicit objections — it became absolutely evident to the "radicals" that Zwingli was on the wrong track. They were convinced that, as a false prophet, he was making inadmissible church-political concessions. God's Word, they declared, is clear and unequivocal: it forbids the abomination of the mass, demands the exclusion of priests (Deut. 12:29–31; 13:1–17), and commands the immediate establishment of a congregation of the faithful. One of the results of this view was their rejection of civil government and of all the political and economic arrangements it protected. In private, Konrad Grebel spoke disparagingly of his erstwhile model Zwingli.

Their ideal of a congregation of the faithful rendered infant baptism questionable as a symbol of membership in the Christian church. The spring of 1524 brought the first rejections of baptism. On August 15, 1524, the Council insisted on the obligation to baptize all newborn infants. Zwingli secretly — and in vain — conferred with the opponents of baptism, who entered into relations with the opponents of Luther in the summer of 1524. But their connection with Andreas Carlstadt, and especially with Thomas Muentzer, did not have any influence on the emerging Anabaptist movement in Zurich. Although tension between Zwingli and the Grebel group became increasingly obvious, the open break was postponed until the beginning of 1525.

Late in 1524, the Council called for official discussions between the people's priests and the radicals, but these were soon broken off. As a result, Zwingli drew a sharp line of separation from them in his *Whoever Causes Unrest (Wer Ursache gebe zu Aufruhr)*. At this point, government was forced to act. Again it made use of the tried and true method of a disputation in order to resolve a pending religious issue.

On January 17, 1525, opponents of infant baptism were required to defend their position, on the basis of Scripture, in public debate. According to the councilmen's verdict, the defense was unsuccessful; a decree declaring their position heretical appeared the very next day, adding that infants must be baptized and that anyone refusing to obey would have to leave the territory of Zurich. A decision to deport four non-Zurich residents followed shortly thereafter. The Zurich natives Grebel and Felix Manz remained unmolested for the moment, but they were warned to refrain from public debates and to give up their private meetings.

In order to realize their ideal of community, the radicals ignored these measures. On January 21, 1525, they performed the first adult baptisms, and founded their own Anabaptist community shortly afterward in Zollikon — a village that was supported in typical fashion by the Great Minster Foundation, and in which refusals to pay the tithe had occurred very early on. The deported Anabaptists moved into adjacent territories and engaged in lively missionary activity in Schaffhausen and St. Gallen.

The organized Anabaptist groups thus established intended, in imitation of Christ, to realize the model of the early Christian community described in Acts. "Public" worship services were rejected and replaced by "private" meetings with discussions about the Bible.

At the heart of these meetings was the call to confession and to penance. Adult baptism was practiced as the sign of conversion. Love was to be the only ruler in these communities, all forms of coercion were rejected, and the secular-civil legal system was repudiated. This attitude was expressed in their refusal to take any oath or to perform any governmental duties, and, ultimately, in their use of the ban. The members of this fraternity delimited themselves sharply from their environment by exercising strict control over their members on the one hand, and, in cases of misbehavior, by exclusion measures conforming to Matt. 18:15–17; on the other hand, they radically limited outside social contacts of their members. For example, one no longer greeted outsiders, no longer lived with them, and no longer shared the same table with people of the world. To appeal to worldly courts was considered in especially bad taste. But there was no question of any plans for the violent overthrow of government or of eschatological threats of judgment. The first spurt of Anabaptist expansion coincided with the peasants' war both chronologically and factually.

Only the most recent research has been able to prove that there is correspondence between Anabaptism and the peasant uprising with regard to chief causes. James Stayer, in particular, has demonstrated their similar aspirations and goals regarding anticlericalism, local autonomy, and disengagement from urban-ecclesiastical guardianship. Earlier documents refer all-inclusively to close personal and organizational connections between Anabaptist leaders and rebellious peasant bands, but such connections cannot be ascertained in Zwingli's vicinity.

What is important is the insight that Anabaptism did not originate solely out of protest against Zurich's government-led church, but instead grew out of a much wider spectrum of social, economic, political, ecclesiastical, and theological factors. Any attempt to derive Anabaptism from a single cause will fail. Still, Anabaptists are without doubt most indebted to Zwingli as far as theology is concerned; to that extent they can be considered his disciples.

It is true that, after some vacillation — at times he himself had doubts about infant baptism — Zwingli very early on recognized his social-political and ecclesiological views as antithetical to the radicals, and set out to defend his views accordingly. When the baptism problem moved into the forefront during the course of 1524, and in 1525 became the principal mark of identification, Zwingli felt obliged to defend his view of baptism and ecclesiology on several occasions. Unfortunately, we lack a thorough investigation of his doctrine of baptism.

Zwingli used *On Baptism, Anabaptism, and Infant Baptism (Von der Taufe, von der Wiedertaufe und von der Kindertaufe)*[1] as a con-

tribution to the discussions in late 1524 and to the January 1525 disputation. This treatise disclosed his deep dismay over the conflict
with his erstwhile followers.

Zwingli's theology of baptism attacked on two fronts: first, traditional doctrine erred when it ascribed sin-expunging power to the
sacrament of baptism and especially to baptismal water. By applying
the principle that nothing external can purify us or justify us,[2] Zwingli
repudiated baptism as a means of grace, in contrast to both traditional church doctrine and to Luther. He declared that baptism, like
the Lord's Supper, is a sign and therefore can effect nothing. Zwingli
shared with the Anabaptists a rejection of the traditional concept of
baptism and a concept of the sacrament as symbol: baptism
announces that the baptized belong to God, that they intend to
arrange their life accordingly, and that they will follow Christ; baptism stands at the beginning of a path. For the Anabaptists, however,
baptism symbolized the change that has already occurred in one's life
and one's commitment to a new existence in the Christian community.

But, since Zwingli also saw—albeit less strongly—an element of
commitment before God on the part of the baptized, infant baptism
presented him with a special problem. How can a minor enter into
such a covenant? Zwingli essentially defended infant baptism with
two arguments: infant baptism is neither commanded nor prohibited
in the Bible; but since the sacraments of the new covenant were first
created in the Old Testament symbols of circumcision and passover,
baptism should be conferred on infants. According to the testimony
of Scripture, the children of Christians belong to God; this belonging
should be expressed by baptism. Moreover, infant baptism committed
children to a Christian life style and committed parents to a corresponding education.[3] Once again Zwingli expressed ecclesiological
reservations: the practice of adult baptism leads to the isolation of a
group of people deeming themselves sinless, and therefore they must
be accused of not being ready to assume responsibility for the well-
being of the community—in fact, the Zurich city-state—as a whole.

Zwingli repeated this viewpoint in his *Response to Balthasar Hub-
maier's Booklet on Baptism (Antwort über Balthasar Hubmaiers
Taufbüchlein)*,[4] in which he attacked the best theologically educated

mind of the Anabaptists, a former professor of theology in Ingolstadt who was staying in Zurich temporarily. He finished it just in time for another disputation on baptism in Zurich.[5] The Anabaptist movement could not be repressed, in spite of this theological counterattack and the more severe measures undertaken by the Zurich government — going as far as the execution by drowning of Manz on January 5, 1527 — so that even the delegates of the Protestant cities conferred about a possible defense against them in the summer of 1527.

It is in this connection that Zwingli once again and conclusively grappled with Anabaptism in *Refutation of the Schemes of the Anabaptists (In catabaptistarum strophas elenchus).*[6] This time the issue for Zwingli was a theological-scientific invalidation of the Anabaptist standpoint. On the basis of Anabaptist written testimony (for example, the Schleitheim Articles of February 24, 1527) Zwingli compared their views, point by point, to his own. There were no discernible shifts from his earlier statements, except that he now supported his argument that children already belong to God by elaborating the covenant idea:[7] God renewed with Abraham the same covenant he had made with Noah; he commanded Abraham to circumcise, as a sign that even children too young to understand are included in this covenant. The same covenant God had thus made with Israel he also made with Christians, so as to render them and Israel one people and one church. A single covenant unites the Old and the New Testaments — only a relative difference separates them.

Zwingli tied election to his covenant idea. Like the establishment of the covenant, election precedes faith and in fact makes faith possible; therefore, if the Anabaptists required faith as a prerequisite to church membership, they reversed — in inadmissible fashion — the God-instituted order of covenant- election- inclusion in God's people-faith.

The harsh measures employed by the authorities both within and outside the Confederation after 1527–1528 did succeed in damming Anabaptist activity somewhat, so that organized Anabaptism, as an alternative to the Zwinglian Reformation, had almost totally disappeared from the territory of Zurich by the end of Zwingli's life.

The start of a periodically convened Synod coincided with the repulsion of Anabaptism. In the fall of 1527, the Council concluded that there was still a large amount of diversity in the teaching of the preachers, and that their life style also left much to be desired. As a corrective measure, a decree dated April 8, 1528 required all preachers to report in person to Zurich twice a year, and to bring along one or two honorable men from their congregations who would be given an opportunity to discuss their pastor's teaching and morals.

The first thus constituted Synod was convened under Zwingli's chairmanship on April 21, 1528 in the Zurich city hall. The pastors were required to take an oath that they would commit themselves to preach the gospel, exercise moral discipline, and obey the authorities.[8] In accordance with Synod rules,[9] every clergyman had to leave the room in turn so as to provide his congregational representatives an opportunity to present their complaints; the pastor was then recalled and informed of the verdict by Zwingli. This practice of so-called grading (*Zensur*) was maintained in Zurich for a long time.

The Synod had no executive powers, but eight councilmen attended the sessions to initiate any actions that might be required. The assembly could also go to them with suggestions concerning other ecclesiastical matters. All disciplinary and legislative powers remained in the hands of civil authorities.

In conclusion, the following are the essential points for judging Zwingli's conflict with the Anabaptists:

1. One can speak of "Anabaptists" only after 1525, when practical consequences followed from doubts about infant baptism which had been expressed for some time. Zwingli found this conflict particularly painful for humane as well as objective reasons.

2. The Anabaptists were convinced they had taken Zwingli's program of reform seriously, and that Zwingli, on the other hand, had become untrue to himself when he clung to infant baptism and defended the rights of government in matters of faith. Zwingli, they asserted, had not really broken completely with the papal church. These two charges must have hit Zwingli particularly hard, since they were accusations of pliability and vacillation which at the same time reproached him with exactly the same thing he himself had used against Lutherans—in his eyes the Lutherans still dragged around Catholic remnants with regard to the other sacrament.

3. Zwingli did not consider the question of adult baptism one of the chief problems. He was much more concerned about the underly-

ing issue of authority involved in decisions of faith, and thus about ecclesiology. From the very beginning, Zwingli defended the Large Council's full authority to make decisions as representative of the parish. Zwingli had to regard any opposition to this fundamental idea as endangering the achievement of his Reformation.

4. There is no discernible evidence to show that Zwingli experienced any decisive change of mind in his assessment of the government's role.

5. Anabaptist theology opposed Zwingli's coordination of human and divine righteousness. It broke up that balanced relationship in favor of translating divine righteousness into reality.

6. The Anabaptists, with similar oversimplification, dissolved Zwingli's synopsis of the Old and New Testaments in the covenant concept, and replaced it with their partiality for the New Testament.

2. The Lord's Supper Controversy

Zwingli's earliest remarks on the sacrament of the altar stem perhaps from his pre-Zurich period, and can be found in his notes in his copy of Augustine's interpretation of the Gospel of John.[10] In imitation of Erasmus, Zwingli stressed the communal character of the sacrament and, refuting Augustine, he declared that the sixth chapter of the Gospel of John (v. 53–56) referred to spiritual eating and drinking.

The next available statements date from 1522, when Zwingli, in his response to Bishop Hugo, casually denied that the celebration of the mass serves to expunge punishment for sins.[11] These limited allusions were expanded the following year into a detailed critique of traditional teaching and practice of the mass, in the eighteenth *Concluding Statement*[12] and its interpretation.[13] Zwingli asserted that, since Christ had paid for all the sins of humankind with his unique sacrifice on the cross, no sacrifice has been possible since then; therefore the mass is not a sacrifice but a remembrance of this one sacrifice and an assurance of the salvation proffered through Christ. By thus rejecting the predominant concept of the mass, Zwingli did not really distinguish himself from Luther or other Reformation critics. Only in 1525 did clear differences appear, when the issue was to determine the manner of Christ's presence in the Eucharist.

Luther never doubted the presence of Christ's body and blood in the elements (real presence). Moreover, real presence gained increased significance in his Lord's Supper teaching after 1523, especially after it led to a break between himself and his Wittenberg colleague Andreas Carlstadt, who had emphatically rejected the real presence. In late 1524, when Carlstadt published three pamphlets on the Lord's Supper in Basel and received the approval of John Oecolampadius and Zwingli, word got around very quickly, and of course Luther heard about it.

The entire relationship between Luther and Zwingli was determined by this event. The Wittenberger regarded Zwingli as primarily a partisan of his erstwhile colleague and present opponent Carlstadt. According to the latter's teaching on the sacrament, the celebration of the Lord's Supper is a congregation's confessional act in which the death of Christ is proclaimed. In line with John 6:63 ("It is the Spirit that gives life, the flesh is of no avail"), Carlstadt taught that the body and blood of Christ are eaten spiritually. At the end of January 1525, Luther settled his accounts with Carlstadt in the treatise *Against the Heavenly Prophets. In the Matter of Images and Sacraments.* According to Luther, only the real presence guarantees the Lord's Supper as a means to transmit salvation.

Zwingli acquired the insight essential to his concept of the Lord's Supper during the second half of 1524. The issue was the meaning of the words of institution, "This is my body, this is my blood." Zwingli was certain of the spiritual character of the Lord's Supper on the basis of the Gospel of John. He stated that that is why the word of institution "is" must not be taken literally; instead, it must be interpreted in the sense of "signifies." Jesus meant to say that bread and wine "signified" body and blood, just as they were sacrificed on the cross for the salvation of humanity. The eucharistic elements are signs pointing to salvation and liberation, but they themselves do not bring them. Zwingli took this interpretation of "is" from a treatise by the Dutch humanist Cornelius Hoehn.

Zwingli rejected the sacrament as means of salvation. In 1525, he expressed his newly acquired insights regarding the sacrament of the altar in several scholarly treatises, without referring to his real debating opponent, Luther, by name. In November 1524 he wrote a *Letter to Matthew Alber Regarding the Lord's Supper (Ad Mattheum Albe-*

rum de coena dominica epistola).[14] The *Commentary (Commentarius)*, with its section *On the Eucharist (de Eucharistia)* was also published that month;[15] *On the Eucharist* was published separately soon afterward. In August 1525, Zwingli published the treatise *Rearguard and Final Flourish with Regard to the Lord's Supper (Subsidium sive coronis de eucharistia)*[16] as a supplement. Three months later, he argued against the Lutheran Bugenhagen in *Response to the Letter of John Bugenhagen (Responsio ad epistolam Ioannis Bugenhagii).*[17]

The contrast between Luther's understanding of the Lord's Supper and that of Zwingli and Oecolampadius became more and more obvious. The factions that developed as a result of the split made special efforts to win over South German forces friendly to the Reformation to their side. This resulted in a new phase of scholarly controversy. In February 1526, Zwingli addressed the laity in the German treatise *A Clear Briefing About Christ's Supper (Eine klare Unterrichtung vom Nachtmahl Christi),*[18] first attacking the teaching of the real presence and then defending his own symbolic understanding. Zwingli advanced empirical, exegetical, and dogmatic arguments against the real presence:

1. If the word "is" had to be taken literally, the real body and blood would then be really seen and tasted. Invisible corporeality is sheer nonsense.

2. Like Erasmus, Zwingli again argued on the basis of John 6:63: our earthly, visible, material world ("flesh") cannot be the bearer of the salvation-bringing Spirit; everything in it — the oral word spoken by human beings as well as the elements of the Lord's Supper — points away from itself toward another, higher, salvation-bringing reality ("Spirit"). Jesus used earthly images as parables for the spiritual and the heavenly; the same applies to Jesus' saying about eating flesh and drinking blood in John 6. It is a matter of a parable pointing to a spiritual-religious event: just as eating and drinking strengthen the body, so does Jesus' submission on the cross feed the soul. The words of institution must be understood as metaphor, and the Lord's Supper is an event that substitutes for the imperceptible spiritual occurrence. That is why Zwingli's understanding was called "symbolic" interpretation.

3. His dogmatic argument started with the same presupposition and applies the sharp distinction between the divine and the human to the God-Man Jesus Christ, too. The two natures of Christ are sharply separated; biblical statements referring to only one nature can be applied only to that nature. No transference or fusion of the two natures occurs. Thus Zwingli rejected the doctrine of the "communication of attributes" (communicatio idiomatum). When Scripture refers to Christ's ascension and second coming, these statements apply only to his human nature, for, according to his divine nature, Christ is with the Father (John 1:18). Since Christ is bodily in heaven after his ascension, he cannot be bodily present in the elements of the Lord's Supper. Zwingli denied the doctrine of ubiquity: like every human being, Christ too is prevented from being in more than one place at a time.

In his positive assessment of the Lord's Supper, Zwingli again dealt with the metaphorical character of biblical statements in detail. Even though he rejected the real presence, he did not simply deny the presence of the gift of salvation. However, he did transfer its presence into the hearts of believers, who are stimulated through the celebration of the Lord's Supper to remember with gratitude the suffering and death of Christ. The aspect of remembrance is more to him than a mere looking back, since the platonically apprehended intimate relationship between the remembering subject and the remembered object resonates in Zwingli's understanding of "remembrance" (memoria). Thus a particular kind of presence is effected.[19]

Zwingli found a parallel in the Old Testament for this essential element of the sacrament, just as he had for baptism: the lamb is not the focal point of the Passover Feast either; instead, the focal point is the remembrance of having been graciously preserved, God's gracious gift that is effective until the present day. This memory arouses gratitude, which is why Zwingli clung to the term "Eucharist" and preferred to use the term "act of thanksgiving" (gratiarum actio) in Latin, rather than "sacrament" (sacramentum).

The two other positive aspects of Zwingli's description of the Lord's Supper were less important in this treatise: the celebration of the Lord's Supper brings the congregation together; it is a "communal arrangement (gemeine Vereinbarung) of believers."[20] Here again Zwingli relied on Erasmus.[21]

4. Zwingli stressed, as the fourth aspect, that the participants in the Lord's Supper confess their Christian faith and proclaim that they have been saved by Jesus Christ's shedding of blood and death.[22] The congregation pledges itself to follow Jesus. Therefore, at the center of the celebration is the congregation whose faithful remembering recognizes Christ's saving deed behind these external proceedings. Thus the following elements formed Zwingli's understanding of the Eucharist: remembering, giving thanks, coming together, confessing, and pledging.

Luther reacted with dismay. The representatives of the symbolic understanding seemed to him to be more dangerous than the pope's adherents. But it was not until the spring of 1527 that he argued extensively with his opponents. In his treatise *That These Words of Christ, 'This is My Body etc.' Still Stand Firm Against the Fanatics (Dass Diese Worte Christi 'Das ist mein Leib etc.' noch fest stehen wider die Schwarmgeister)* it became apparent that, from the very beginning, Luther moved his controversy with Zwingli and his followers into the context of a battle against Satanic forces. The Wittenberger gave the Lord's Supper conflict a religious interpretation.

Conversely, Zwingli fought to destroy the last remnants of traditional doctrine through scholarly argumentation. Luther was convinced that his Reformation work was at stake in the issue of the real presence, which is why his only concern in this and other treatises was the subject of the bodily presence of Christ: just as in his incarnation God binds himself to fleshliness, worldliness, and earthliness, so does he want to offer salvation itself in the Lord's Supper in the external forms of bread and wine. Since Luther had in principle overcome the differentiation between sign and substance to which Zwingli clung — in the wake of Augustine — he considered Zwingli's interpretation of the "is" recidivism.

The literary controversy, in which — besides Luther and Zwingli — Martin Bucer, Oecolampadius, and other theologians from Upper Germany took part, dragged on until 1528. Its proceedings need not be described here, since it did not introduce any important new points.

When the political situation for the Protestants worsened in 1528, there were increased efforts to build bridges between the Lutheran and the Zwinglian views in order to help unite the antipapal forces.

The impetus for such a compromise came from Strasbourg. Wolfgang Capito and Bucer strove to achieve concord, and supported the plan to eliminate contradictions through an academic disputation.

Bucer mediated between Zwingli and Luther. With the Zuricher, he rejected the real presence and emphasized the spiritual usufruct; with Luther, he acknowledged a saving gift to the soul in the Lord's Supper. The Hessian Duke Philip was working for a political coalition of all Protestant forces, which is why he seized upon the plan to hold a theological discussion as a means of achieving unity and invited the dueling parties to Marburg. Zwingli accepted the invitation to participate because he was still counting on being able to convince Luther, and rode cheerfully to Hesse. The Wittenberger, however, did not expect anything to come out of such a meeting, and had to be urged to attend by his duke.

Accompanied by Oecolampadius, Zwingli arrived in Marburg on September 28, 1529, and on the following day preached to a large audience about predestination.[23] Luther and Melanchthon arrived somewhat later. Besides these principal disputants, theologians from Wittenberg, Strasbourg, Ulm, Nuremberg, and Halle also participated.

No transcript exists of the proceedings of the debates held from October 1–3, but the various reports by the participants do present an adequate picture.[24] No new aspects were discussed beyond the points already expressed in written form. The discussions of the theologians reached an impasse, and only at the urging of the political authorities did the churchmen compose a list of common convictions of faith. The Zwinglians added a few sentences to a text based on one of Luther's suggestions; these sentences firmly fixed the Holy Spirit as the mediator of salvation.

The resulting fifteen *Marburg Articles*[25] established common teaching in fourteen articles: trinity, immaculate conception, Christ's work of salvation, faith, preaching, baptism, good works, private confession, political authority, ecclesiastical customs. The fifteenth article established the differences in their responses to the question of Christ's presence in the Lord's Supper.

Each side was afterward convinced it had overcome the other. When he preached from the Great Minster pulpit after his return,

Zwingli himself gave the *Marburg Articles* an interpretation that he must have known the Lutherans would never have affirmed.[26] The Marburg Colloquy was a political mistake, and, even ecclesiastically, produced only an abatement of public controversy without lessening the contrariety.

There is insufficient research to show to what extent Zwingli's understanding of the Lord's Supper changed after the Marburg Colloquy. Stefan Niklaus Bosshard dealt most extensively with this phase, and he noticed a "real development"[27] in the older Zwingli. Bosshard highlighted specific parallels with Zwingli's understanding of the Lord's Supper before his conflict with Luther; and he stressed Zwingli's enduring agreements with Erasmus. Whenever Zwingli addressed Catholics in his later confessional writings, he paid greater attention to the effect of the celebration and of the elements on the inner person. By capturing the senses of the participants in the sacrament, and by directing them to what is real, the elements have been assigned a supportive role in the "faithful contemplation" (*contemplatio fidei*)[28] of Christ's act of salvation. The Lord's Supper has become a "theater of salvation" (*theatrum salutis*) which, however, imparts something only to those who already have faith. Such a faith can be strengthened through the Lord's Supper. Zwingli never ceased repudiating any faith-creating function of the sacrament. The question is whether there are connecting links between Zwingli's "faithful contemplation" and late medieval meditations on the sacrament.

In conclusion, five points are highlighted for any assessment of Zwingli's doctrine of the Lord's Supper, as well as for the eucharistic controversy as a whole:

1. Zwingli and Luther—either covertly or overtly—had already taken divergent theological positions even before the eucharistic controversy. Their greatest difference concerned the way salvation was mediated.

2. For this reason, the eucharistic controversy cannot be understood as a process of disuniting. It is much more a matter of a process that revealed ever more extensive divergences; at the same time, it led to the formation of Protestant confessional parties.

3. Zwingli and Luther each assessed the conflict differently. Zwingli championed further development of the Reformation, and

attempted to convince his challenger. Until the Marburg Colloquy, he counted on being able to win the opposition party over to his side. Luther, on the other hand, regarded his conflict with Zwingli as a continuation of his fight with Carlstadt. He considered the denial of the real presence solely an attack by the devil, to whom the deluded succumb.

4. Any assessment of inner-Protestant contrarieties must not lose sight of the frequently forgotten fact that Zwingli never cast eyes on Luther until the eucharistic controversy, and that Luther's encounter with Zwingli was limited to that event.

5. In an extension of these circumstances, as it were, any treatment of Zwingli's theology until well into the twentieth century frequently focused on his teachings about the sacrament, particularly on his criticisms of other views of the Eucharist. This does not do justice to the Zurich reformer, because it overlooks his positive statements regarding the sacrament and because it does not see their connection with Zwingli's theology.

3. Bibliography

The Argument with Anabaptists

Blanke, Fritz. *Brüder in Christo. Die Geschichte der ältesten Täufergemeinde (Zollikon 1525).* Zurich, 1955.
————. *Brethren in Christ. The History of the Oldest Anabaptist Congregation.* Translated by Joseph Nordenhaug. Scottsdale, Pa., 1961.
Fast, Heinold. "Bemerkungen zur Taufanschauung der Täufer." *Archiv für Reformationsgeschichte* 57 (1966): 131–51.
————. " 'Die Wahrheit wird euch freimachen.' Die Anfänge der Täuferbewegung in Zürich in der Spannung zwischen erfahrener und verheissener Wahrheit." *Mennonitische Geschichtsblätter* 32 (1975): 7–33.
Gerner, Gottfried. "Folgerungen aus dem täuferischen Gebrauch der Heiligen Schrift." *Mennonitische Geschichtsblätter* 31 (1974): 25–43.
Goertz, Hans Jürgen, ed., *Umstrittenes Täufertum, 1525–1975. Neue Forschungen.* 2d ed. Gottingen, 1977.
————. *Die Täufer. Geschichte und Deutung.* Munich, 1980.
Stayer, James M. *Anabaptists and the Sword.* Lawrence, Kansas, 1972.
————, Werner O. Packull, and Klaus Deppermann. "From Monogenesis to Polygenesis. The Historical Discussion of Anabaptist Origins." *Mennonite Quarterly Review* 49 (1975): 83–121.

————. "Die Schweizer Brüder. Versuch einer historischen Definition." *Mennonitische Geschichtsblätter* 34 (1977): 7–34.

Usteri, Johann Martin. "Darstellung der Tauflehre Zwinglis. (Mit besonderer Berücksichtigung der wiedertäuferischen Streitigkeiten)." *Theologische Studien und Kritiken* 55 (1882): 205–84.

Yoder, John H. *Täufertum und Reformation in der Schweiz.* Vol. 1, *Die Gespräche zwischen Täufern und Reformatoren 1523–1538.* Schriftenreihe des Mennonitischen Geschichtsvereins 6. Karlsruhe, 1962.

————. *Täufertum und Reformation im Gespräch. Dogmengeschichtliche Untersuchung der frühen Gespräche zwischen Schweizerischen Täufern und Reformatoren.* Basler Studien zur historischen und systematischen Theologie 13. Zurich, 1968.

The Lord's Supper Controversy

Bosshard, Stefan Niklaus. *Zwingli-Erasmus-Cajetan. Die Eucharistie als Zeichen der Einheit.* Veröffentlichungen des Instituts für europäische Geschichte Mainz 89. Weisbaden, 1978.

Bühler, Peter. "Der Abendmahlsstreit der Reformatoren und seine aktuellen Implikationen." *Theologische Zeitschrift* 35 (1979): 228–41.

Gäbler, Ulrich. "Luthers Beziehungen zu den Schweizern und Oberdeutschen von 1526 bis 1530/1531." In Helmar Junghans, ed., *Leben und Werk Martin Luthers von 1526 bis 1546. Festgabe zu seinem 500. Geburtstag,* 481–96; 885–91. East Berlin, 1983.

Gollwitzer, Helmut. "Zur Auslegung von Joh. 6 bei Luther und Zwingli." In Werner Schmauch, ed., *In Memoriam Ernst Lohmeyer,* 143–68. Stuttgart, 1951.

Grötzinger, Eberhard. *Luther und Zwingli. Die Kritik an der mittelalterlichen Lehre von der Messe — als Wurzel des Abendmahlsstreits.* Okumenische Theologie 5. Zurich and Cologne: Gütersloh, 1980.

Hausammann, Susi. "Die Marburger Artikel — eine echte Konkordie?" *Zeitschrift für Kirchengeschichte* 77 (1966): 288–321.

Köhler, Walther. *Zwingli und Luther. Ihr Streit über das Abendmahl nach seinen politischen und religiösen Beziehungen.* 2 vols. Quellen und Forschungen zur Reformationsgeschichte 6 and 7. Leipzig and Gütersloh, 1924 and 1953.

————, ed., *Das Marburger Religionsgespräch 1529. Versuch einer Rekonstruktion.* Schriften des Vereins für Reformationsgeschichte 148. Leipzig, 1929.

Locher, Gottfried W. *Streit unter Gästen. Die Lehre aus der Abendmahlsdebatte der Reformatoren für das Verständnis und die Feier des Abendmahls heute.* Theologische Studien 110. Zurich, 1972.

Staedtke, Joachim. "Abendmahl (Reformationszeit/Protestantismus)." In *Theologische Realenzyklopädie,* 1:106–22. Berlin and New York, 1977.

IX

CONFESSION AND POLITICS (1529–1531)

1. Plans for Alliances

After the Confederation's partition along sharply contrasting confessional lines in 1528–1529, Zurich's and Zwingli's connections to non-Confederation theologians and politicians increased. For one thing, it was a matter of having Zwinglianism adopted in the South German cities. But above all, Zurich and its Christian Fortress Law allies were seeking more partners to repulse a possible Hapsburg and Five States threat. The results of the Marburg Colloquy had demonstrated the impossibility of unifying all Protestants. For that reason, both sides set out to form more limited coalitions in October 1529.

For Zwingli and for Zurich the chief goal was an alliance with Duke Philip of Hesse. René Hauswirth investigated this subject and carefully described the complicated connections between Zurich's Confederate and foreign policies and Zwingli's part in them. He was able to document how previous research had overestimated Zwingli's political abilities and opportunities. Zwingli did not possess a wealth of ideas, nor did he have a realistic grasp of the existing balance of power in Europe. Furthermore, Zwingli was not really a full-fledged political partner, since he lacked the means to implement his plans in Zurich.

Zwingli thought that the Hapsburg and papal powers were embodied in the emperor, and that all opposing forces were embodied in young Philip of Hesse. He conducted a lively and private correspondence with Philip in which political plans and goals were discussed. Making a much too optimistic judgment, Zwingli considered Philip a dependable adherent who would prepare the way for his Reformation in Middle and North Germany. Moreover, Zwingli was convinced that an alliance with Hesse would also be advantageous to the Confederate cities, and described these advantages in *Notes Concerning the Advantages of an Alliance with Hesse (Notizen betreffend die Vorteile des hessischen Bündnisses).*[1] Zwingli's concern was to establish firm connections with the outside and to find backing for the implementation of the Reformation in the Confederation itself. Bern refused to participate in these plans for alliances precisely because of these entanglements, and because of possible new difficulties with Savoy.

After laborious negotiations, the cities of Zurich, Basel, and Strasbourg — without the participation of Bern — signed the "Christian Understanding" with Philip of Hesse in November 1530, promising mutual support in case of attack. Zwingli brought to these negotiations with Hesse some grandiose ideas of alliances with other anti-Hapsburg forces. A Zurich envoy did sound out the Venetian doge at the end of December 1529, but suffered a friendly rebuff.

The plans, pursued until 1531, for an alliance with France proved to be equally unrealistic. On a purely diplomatic mission, Zwingli personally negotiated with the authorized French negotiator, since he understood his native tongue. But just how much this assignment was entangled with religious motives was demonstrated by his formulation of a confessional statement intended for the French king's attention. The *Exposition of the Christian Faith (Christianae fidei expositio),*[2] not printed until 1536, was the last link in the chain of Zwingli's summaries of his theology.[3] Zwingli's confession was delivered to Paris by messenger, but there is no record of any reaction to it. The treaty negotiations broke down, because the goals of these unequal partners were too far apart: France wanted to maintain good relations with the Five States.

Michael Gaismaier — who had been driven out of Tyrol, and with whom Zwingli had had contact since 1525–1526 — did prepare an approach to Venice, but had absolutely no access to the kind of power base that would have interested Zurich. Plans to cooperate with Milan also failed.

In the fall of 1529, the Saxon elector had also initiated moves toward an alliance, but its basic requirement was the affirmation of the Lutheran confession. The Upper German cities were faced with a decision forced on them by this polarization. Much to Zwingli's disappointment, eight influential municipalities chose to remain absolutely neutral; only Strasbourg, which joined the Christian Fortress Law on January 5, 1530, chose Zwinglianism.

2. The Augsburg Diet of 1530 and Zwingli's Confessions: *Account of Faith* and *On God's Providence*

When, in January 1530, Emperor Charles V sent invitations to the Augsburg Diet, the Protestants presented an image of confusion. Since the sovereign intended to listen to all religious parties in order to arrive at a verdict on the issue of faith, the various Protestant groups were confronted with the problem of how they wished to obtain a hearing.

The Lutherans disassociated themselves from the South German cities and from the Swiss by way of their Augsburg Confession, which contained explicit anti-Zwinglian barbs; under the leadership of Strasbourg, four Upper German cities submitted their own confession (*Confessio Tetrapolitana*), which was intended to take a position midway between the Lutherans and the Zwinglians.

By the time word that these confessions were being prepared reached the Confederation, it was too late for the Fortress Law cities to prepare a formal confession of their own. Zwingli had probably realized since the beginning of the year that he would probably be expected to draft a confession, but he had made no move to do so. Moreover, he had hoped for a personal invitation to Augsburg from Philip of Hesse, but nothing came of it. Furthermore, the duke endorsed the Lutheran confession, albeit with reservations.

Since Zurich had no intention of going it alone, Zwingli, if he wished his views to be heard at all, had no choice but to submit a private confession. He wrote *Account of Faith (Fidei ratio)*[4] in a few days. The title describes the purpose precisely: as he had already done in other writings, Zwingli intended to render an accounting. He expected a verdict regarding his Reformation convictions from the emperor and from the whole church.[5] That is why he subordinated himself to the authority of Holy Scripture and to that of the church which judges Scripture in accordance with the Spirit.[6] Zwingli thought it was possible to convince the emperor and to wean him away from Catholicism. Hidden behind this view — which can only be called utopian — is his unbroken reliance on his argument's power to convince and convert, and on his basic premise — already mentioned several times — that bad rulers are responsible for the misery of both church and world, and that educating them might bring about changes.

The objectives of the *Account of Faith* are in line with those of his *Exposition of Faith (Expositio fidei)* addressed to the French king. Since the formation of confessions had already progressed so far that Zwingli no longer had to take either the Lutherans or the center groups in Upper Germany into account, he used decisive and powerful formulations with clear demarcations from Catholicism and Lutheranism. Modeled after his first Bern sermon, Zwingli's explanations, in twelve articles, conformed to the articles of the Apostles' Creed.

The doctrine of God (article 1) starts with the uniqueness of God and his qualities of Good, True, Powerful, and then leads to Christology where the two natures of Christ are defined in accordance with traditional dogma and with an obvious barb against Luther's teaching of the exchange of qualities (*communicatio idiomatum*). In the doctrine of reconciliation (article 2) Zwingli introduced a new element not present in his other works. Zwingli had previously taught that God made the Fall possible (*infralapsarism*) but he now asserted that God not only made Adam's Fall possible but effected it (*supralapsarism*). To Zwingli, *infralapsarism* threatened to make God's will for salvation dependent on human behavior, namely, on Adam's Fall, but this was contradictory to God's freedom. Zwingli spoke of reconciliation in this connection. Concurring with Anselm of Canterbury's classic doctrine of satisfaction, he saw Christ's crucifixion as fulfillment of the law; this is how divine righteousness is satisfied, which is why it no longer punishes the sinner. In his goodness, God sent His Son; in Him God's love is revealed. Righteousness and love belong together.

The extolling of Christ's sacrifice as the sole validity was directed against the Catholic theory of the sacrifice of the mass (article 3). In his doctrine of original sin (article 4), Zwingli conceded that human beings must sin because of their natural tendencies. Zwingli did not always formulate the necessity to sin in this way when he stressed sin as conscious act. As compensation for this, as it were, he talked of the election of children — which occurs before any trace of faith — when he dealt with Christ's work of salvation (article 5).

His ecclesiology (article 6), with its threefold definition of church, is in sharp contrast to that of the Anabaptists: an invisible church encompasses all people destined for eternal life; only the faithful can grasp membership in it; they can be certain of membership; whether or not nonbelievers are cast out is outside our ken. All those who can be recognized as Christians by external signs, such as baptism or participation in the Lord's Supper, belong to the visible church; among these Christians, however, there are some who in their hearts deny Christ, but it is impossible to single them out. These visible churches or congregations in one place (for example, in Zurich) together constitute the universal church which does not, however, appear in organized form.

Zwingli's most extensive treatment concerned the sacraments (articles 7 and 8). With an anti-Lutheran and anti-Catholic thrust, he denied their grace-imparting power. Grace precedes the sacrament. Membership (invisible) in the church is made visible in baptism; Christ's act of salvation that has taken place is depicted in the Lord's Supper and realized in the contemplation of faith. The subject of ceremonies (article 9) did not seem very important to Zwingli.

The confession accounted for the office of preaching (article 10) in two ways: although the Holy Spirit does not have to come to human beings during the proclamation — therefore does not bind itself to the word — it is nevertheless given only to those who have been reached by the sermon; "the sermon teaches us about the fact of Christ's death; the Spirit reinforces our acceptance of this fact as personally valid."[7] Thus the preacher prepares the work of the Spirit. The pastor has catechetical and social duties in addition to his duty to teach about Christ's act of salvation. He serves justice and public order with his ethically centered sermons; welfare and care for the sick are also among his duties. Zwingli concluded this section with a sharp attack on the Catholic bishops who neglected their duties — he called them "a tumor."

Government, like the preaching office, is in the service of divine goodness. Neither power is superior to the other. Despite his low opinion of the monarchical form of government, Zwingli granted its validity in conformity with the purpose of Scripture. Nevertheless, he scarcely hesitated to point out how seldom a prince rules with goodness and justice. At the same time, Zwingli defended the right to rebel against a tyrant on Christian grounds. His comments on eschatology (article 12) rejected both the Catholic idea of hellfire and several Anabaptist groups' doctrine of universal forgiveness.

The confession's strong anti-Catholic and anti-Lutheran tone inhibited its effectiveness from the very beginning. The Lutherans did not react officially, but in private they criticized it strongly; Melanchthon thought its author was insane.[8] It cannot be determined whether the emperor ever saw the *Account of Faith.*

In that same month, July, Zwingli's old opponent John Eck published a counterattack, *Refutation of the Articles Zwingli Submitted to the Emperor (Repulsio articulorum Zuinglii Caesareae maiestati oblatorum).* Zwingli responded to it in an open letter to the German princes assembled in Augsburg, in which he again dealt with the doctrine of the sacraments and with the Eucharist in particular.[9]

Even while Zwingli was writing the two items intended for the Augsburg Diet, he was busy on another: *Remembrance of the Sermon About God's Providence (Sermonis de providentia Dei anamnema).*[10] Duke Philip had asked Zwingli in January 1530 to send him the sermon he had preached in Marburg on September 29, 1529. On the basis of this request, Zwingli developed a comprehensive Latin discourse on providence; how much of the original sermon is interwoven in the published text is no longer discernible.

One of the most controversial problems of Zwingli interpretation is the evaluation of the treatise on providence. Fritz Büsser has demonstrated, in a survey,[11] that determinism and pantheism have been discerned in Zwingli's writings;[12] the "rationalist" among the reformers has been seen to derive the necessity of providence logically from his concept of God,[13] and to move, in any case, along the lines of the speculative "Renaissance philosophy."[14] Karl Barth and Emil

Brunner, the representatives of dialectical theology, rejected the treatise as a "foreign body" in Zwingli's work, as having "nothing, but absolutely nothing to do with Christian theology." Conversely, Gottfried W. Locher denied any pantheistic or humanist ideas in Zwingli, and instead spoke of a "fusion of divine Omnipotence with the sole validity of Grace"; he characterized the treatise as a whole as "an attack on the Renaissance belief in chance (*fortuna*) that prevailed in the courts of princes."[15]

Any accurate evaluation of the treatise will have to be based on the following factors:

1. The treatise on providence is not a foreign body in Zwingli's literary work. Implicit presuppositions and focal statements can already be found in earlier writings, for example in the *Commentary*, the *First Bern Sermon*, or in *Account of Faith*.[16]

2. Zwingli joined Luther against Erasmus in denying freedom of the will. He explicitly attacked the main idea in Erasmus's treatise *On Free Will*, namely, that after God the First Cause, human will should be regarded as second cause in the attainment of salvation.

3. Agreement with Luther is confined to this point. The treatise is otherwise permeated with a refutation of chief statements of Lutheran theology, especially of those developed against Erasmus in Luther's *On the Bondage of the Will*.

The treatise on providence presents Zwingli's most detailed, most thorough, and most convincing alternative to Luther's thought. All essential questions are touched upon: the doctrine of God, anthropology, soteriology, ethics, doctrine of the Eucharist, understanding of the Bible. Nowhere else in Zwingli's writings is a wider gulf opened between himself and the Wittenberg reformer. Later research has generally underestimated this anti-Lutheran attitude, yet his contemporary, Martin Bucer, noticed it with displeasure.[17]

4. The sharpest contrast is revealed in their image of God. Zwingli opposed the statements, essential for Luther, about the "hidden" God with the "simplicity" of God whose will can be totally recognized in his revelation. This distinction could be in part a result of the continued influence of the two medieval schools, *via antiqua* (Zwingli) and *via moderna* (Luther).

5. The wealth of humanist material he drew upon, as well as some

individual statements—such as the one regarding the election of morally outstanding pagans[18] or that regarding the beauty of the human body[19]—nevertheless do not permit Zwingli to be classified as Renaissance philosopher. On the whole, it is a matter of independent theological achievement, which cannot be squeezed into any existing tradition. However, note must be taken of how closely Zwingli was tied to the Thomistic world view.

6. When asking what Zwingli's purpose was in writing the treatise on providence, events of the time and people he addressed must be taken into consideration. Zwingli's purpose was to deliver a scholarly explanation of his fundamental theological views to Philip of Hesse and others who were vacillating between Zwinglianism and Lutheranism. Developments in 1529 and 1530 must have reinforced Zwingli's conviction that a compromise with Lutherans was no longer possible. That is why he formulated his thoughts without considering them at all, as was the case with *Account of Faith.*

Zwingli was unable to prevent Philip of Hesse from joining other Lutheran princes in the Smalcald League at the end of 1530. The cities favoring Zwingli—Strasbourg, Constance, Memmingen, and Lindau—were also granted membership in the league on the basis of a Lutheran interpretation of the Tetrapolitan Confession. In face of this leniency, even Zurich, Basel, and Bern applied for membership in the league. But Zwingli found this confessional basis to be so totally contradictory to his own view of the Lord's Supper that he refused to join, couching his refusal in extremely harsh terms to Bucer and Wolfgang Capito, who were participating in a conference on this subject in Basel.[20] The plan was dropped.

This repudiation of the Tetrapolitan Confession offended Philip of Hesse as well as the Upper German cities, and relations with the Smalcald League were severed. It marked a step toward isolation in foreign affairs; the Fortress Law cities were forced to implement their own political plans in the Confederation without external protection to their rear.

3. From the First to the Second Kappel War

The results of the First Kappel War permitted Zurich to implement the Reformation according to the congregation principle in a large part of the Common Lordships; most of this activity was concentrated in East Switzerland (Thurgau and Rheintal).

A particular problem was posed by the ecclesiastical territory of the venerable princely abbey of St. Gallen and its extensive landholdings. The convent held the status of Affiliated State within the Confederation. In the fifteenth century, the abbot had signed a defense treaty with Zurich, Lucerne, Glarus, and Schwyz, in order to safeguard his sovereignty against the city of St. Gallen. The protectors, for their part, had been granted extensive political and legal rights "which pushed the 'God House State' almost down to the rank of a Common Lordship."[21]

When reformatory tendencies became noticeable in the abbot's territory, Zurich — basing its case on theological and legal expert opinions — took the position that the congregation principle should be applied in this territory just as in the Common Lordships, and that the sovereignty of the convent should be revoked if need be. Lucerne and Schwyz, its decidedly Catholic treaty partners, repudiated this legal position and several times demanded the appointment of a Confederation court of arbitration. The Zurich government rejected that legal procedure and instead tolerated the expulsion of the abbot, the sale of the convent, and the secularization of the ecclesiastical territory. In the eyes of contemporaries, Zurich was exposed as a brutal lawbreaker.

Despite this Reformation victory in the Common Lordships and in St. Gallen, Zwingli was no nearer his real political-religious goal of Reformation in the Five States at the end of 1530. From the beginning of 1530, he had concentrated increasingly on this task. According to Zwingli's interpretation of the First Peace Treaty, the Catholic states were obligated to permit the "free preaching of the gospel" in their own territories. Seen in practical terms, this would mean that reformatory statements in the congregations must not be suppressed. Zwingli's chief demand was that God's Word must be allowed to be heard. The reformer expected that scriptural sermons would open the eyes of the vassals and lead them to overthrow the ruling, exploiting pension receivers. His trust in the converting power of sermons was unbroken.

The Zurich government adopted Zwingli's whole interpretation of the Peace Treaty. Since the Five States continued to suppress all attempts to reform, and slandered the Protestants, they were portrayed as peace violators, giving the Fortress Law states a lever with which to apply pressure on their Catholic fellow Confederates.

Disagreement arose with regard to the form this pressure should take. Whereas Basel and Schaffhausen wanted to proceed with as much consideration as possible, and Bern — as it had done before — took a middle position, Zurich thought an armed conflict inevitable. Zwingli unequivocally advocated an armed attack on the Five States.[22] So did Leo Jud. The pacifist ideal they had previously espoused had had to give way to the political Reformation goal. The political power play between the Fortress Law cities was made even more confusing by factions within the individual treaty partner states, to say nothing of the foreign connections already mentioned.

In the first part of his investigation of the Kappel War, Helmut Meyer described these events of 1531 in detail; these are some highlights:

Bern prevailed: in May 1531, Zurich reluctantly agreed to merely set up a food blockade against the Five States. At a time already burdened with high prices, this blockade was intended to cut the interior states off from their necessary import of salt, and thus arouse the resentment of the common people, forcing the Catholic states either to give in or go to war. No one in Zurich doubted they themselves would be victorious if it came to war.

The blockade failed miserably. As the arbitration negotiations progressed, the Catholics appeared more and more self-confident; by the beginning of October 1531, Bern drew the only correct conclusion possible and the blockade was withdrawn. Zurich reacted with consternation and urged its continuation. Instead of forcing the Five States to their knees, the Fortress Law cities quarreled among themselves and their alliance was near collapse.

At this point, the Five States made their move and formally declared war on Zurich on October 9, 1531. Their rapid advance shortly thereafter exposed the cities of the Christian Fortress Law in a "state of disorientation":[23] mobilization was proceeding very slowly in Zurich, and military leaders were incompetent.

In any case, on October 11, 1531, thirty-five hundred badly deployed Zurich men faced nearly double that number of Interior

Swiss near Kappel. The battle was decided in a relatively short encounter lasting less than one hour; five hundred Zurichers, among them twenty-five clerics, lost their lives; about one hundred Catholic men died.

Why so many pastors went into battle this time, compared to the First Kappel War, is not answered in the sources. All these clergymen could hardly have been military chaplains, as was said of Zwingli on no evidence whatever. Much more likely is the assumption that the clergy, who were the most vociferous supporters in Zurich of the war, drew the consequences of their attitude and went to war with no formal responsibilities. There is no doubt whatever that Zwingli took an active part in the battle and was killed there.

In conclusion, there should be a response to the question of how much Zwingli influenced politics in this decisive year of 1531. In general, a shift among Zurich's political authorities could be seen: the Large Council repressed the Small Council even more,[24] but, since this numerically large body was incapable of making fast decisions, the executive committee of mayors and master craftsmen gained in importance. Even though the Large Council retained the final say, political affairs — especially foreign policy — were in fact carried on by this committee. Since its members were usually called "secret ones" or "secret counselors," the existence of a legally appointed privy council whose members — Zwingli among them — held all the power was assumed by everyone.

The research of Haas, Jacob, Spillmann, Hauswirth, Meyer, and von Muralt has demonstrated that such a privy council did not exist as a fixed institution with clearly defined powers, although it is apparent that the secret ones, having very little turnover in personnel, had the duty to review incoming news and to prepare suitable laws by way of, for example, writing expert opinions. Foreign policy officials would then carry out these policies, after the Large Council had voted on them. Since the group of foreign policy officials and the "secret ones" overlapped, the "secret ones" "could appear as an agency acting with total independence."[25] To this extent, Ekkehart Fabian is correct when he contrasts the "secret ones" to the Large Council as being decision makers in their own way. However, the actual reality of the situation in Zurich eludes any description in constitutional terms, which are derived from a clear determination of powers.

Zwingli's political activity was carried on in the framework of these committees. The available sources impede any assessment of Zwingli's effectiveness and actual influence in the committees; only four items in his handwriting have been preserved from this period. But one indication is the number of times he was appointed to these committees.

Helmut Meyer has prepared a list of expert opinions and letters, dated from 1531 and 1532, from the privy councils and foreign policy commissions.[26] Of the twenty-one recommendations to the Large Council prepared during Zwingli's lifetime, the composition of the commission responsible for them is known in seventeen cases. Among the total of sixteen commissioners there was not a single pastor except for Zwingli. He was one of the commissioners in thirteen cases; only three councilmen participated more often in preparing recommendations. Thus Zwingli stood out even among politicians.

Whether or to what extent Zwingli's concrete suggestions were adopted cannot be determined with certainty. In any case, there was no obvious opponent to Zwingli's general course of action on the executive board, and yet the Council several times rejected recommendations of the committees. At the end of July 1531, Zwingli himself felt so rejected that he submitted his resignation and was only persuaded to stay on by a delegation of important councilmen.

This much can be said: In contrast to earlier periods of his life, Zwingli took a larger part in purely political affairs in the years 1530 and 1531. The Great Minster pastor produced ideas and arguments for Zurich's foreign policy after the First Kappel War and he influenced Zurich's goals greatly, without, however, being able to determine their actual form.

4. Bibliography

Fabian, Ekkehart. *Geheime Räte in Zürich, Bern, Basel und Schaffhausen. Quellen und Untersuchungen zur Staatskirchenrechts-und Verfassungsgeschichte der Alten Eidgenossenschaft (einschliesslich der Zürcher Notstandsverfassung)*. Schriften zur Kirchen- und Rechtsgeschichte 33. Cologne and Vienna, 1974.

Haas, Martin. "Zwingli und die 'Heimlichen Räte.' " *Zwingliana* 12 (1964): 93–136.

Hauswirth, René. *Landgraf Philipp von Hessen und Zwingli. Voraussetzungen und Geschichte der politischen Beziehungen zwischen Hessen, Strassburg, Konstanz, Ulrich von Württemberg und reformierten Eidgenossen 1526–1531.* Schriften zur Kirchen- und Rechtsgeschichte 35. Tübingen and Basel, 1968.

Jacob, Walter. "Zwingli und 'der' Geheime Rat. Entgegnung an Ekkehart Fabian." *Zwingliana* 13 (1970): 234–44.

Klaassen, Walter. *Michael Gaismair. Revolutionary and Reformer.* Studies in Medieval and Reformation Thought 23. Leiden, 1978.

Köhler, Walther. "Zu Zwinglis französischen Bündnisplänen." *Zwingliana* 4 (1925): 302–11.

———. "Zwingli und Italien." In *Aus fünf Jahrhunderten Schweizerische Kirchengeschichte. Zum 60. Geburtstag von Paul Wernle*, 22–28. Basel, 1932.

———. "Der Augsburger Reichstag und die Schweiz." *Schweizerische Zeitschrift für Geschichte* 3 (1953): 169–89.

Locher, Gottfried W. "Die Prädestinationslehre Huldrych Zwinglis." In *Huldrych Zwingli in neuer Sicht*, 105–25. Zurich and Stuttgart, 1969.

———. "Zu Zwinglis 'Professio fidei.' Beobachtungen und Erwägungen zur Pariser Reinschrift der sogenannten Fidei Expositio." *Zwingliana* 12 (1968): 689–700.

Meyer, Helmut. *Der Zweite Kappeler Krieg. Die Krise der Schweizerischen Reformation.* Zurich, 1976.

Muralt, Leonhard von. "Zum Problem der Theokratie bei Zwingli." In *Discordia Concors. Festschrift für Edgar Bonjour*, 2: 367–90. Basel and Stuttgart, 1968.

Pfister, Rudolf. *Das Problem der Erbsünde bei Zwingli.* Quellen und Abhandlungen zur Schweizerischen Reformationsgeschichte 9. Leipzig, 1939.

———. *Die Seligkeit erwählter Heiden bei Zwingli. Eine Untersuchung zu seiner Theologie.* Zollikon and Zurich, 1952.

Rother, Siegfried. *Die religiösen und geistigen Grundlagen der Politik Huldrych Zwinglis. Ein Beitrag zum Problem des christlichen Staates.* Erlanger Abhandlungen zur mittleren und neueren Geschichte 7. Erlangen, 1956.

Spillmann, Kurt. *Zwingli und die zürerische Politik gegenüber der Abtei St. Gallen.* Mitteilungen zur Vaterländischen Geschichte 44. St. Gallen, 1965.

———. "Zwingli und Zurich nach dem Ersten Landfrieden." *Zwingliana* 12 (1965): 254–80; 12 (1966): 309–29.

Straub, Franz. "Zürich und die Bewährung des Ersten Landfrieden (Herbst 1529 bis Herbst 1530)." Ph.D. diss., Zurich, 1970.

X
ZWINGLI'S HISTORICAL IMPACT

1. The Problem

Any investigation of Zwingli's historical impact must begin with the question of whether Zwingli's work really revealed such typical traits that it could be classified as source material beyond doubt. There is no unity in Zwingli research about what really constitutes the essence of Zwingli's theology and what distinguishes it from that of others. One glance at the most recent summaries of his theology, for example, by Locher, Courvoisier, Neuser, or Gestrich, shows how large the disparity can be in general and in particular. If there is so much uncertainty about Zwingli himself, how can the aftereffects of this Zwinglianism be established?[1] Inquiry into his historical impact is therefore intimately tied to Zwingli interpretation itself. Until now there has been little awareness of these difficulties.

The most extensive treatment of aftereffects has been by Locher, who tried to go beyond merely describing the dissemination of Zwingli writings and the study of them. It is true that in his summary of Zwingli's theology[2] Locher no longer referred in typical fashion to "Zwinglianism" or something like it; instead, he spoke of "the theological character of the Zurich Reformation," which is the appropriate way to express the fact that Zwingli's theology cannot really be delineated without taking the developments in Zurich into consideration. Moreover, under the heading "Character and Particularity of the Zurich Reformation," Locher combined the era of Zwingli and that of his successor Heinrich Bullinger (1504–1575). He also used the term "late Zwinglianism" for Bullinger's era, to express the shifts in individualization and in institutionalization. Staedtke was right when he asked whether it would not be more accurate to call it "Bullingerism" rather than "late Zwinglianism."[3]

In any case, this terminological lack of clarity derives from a further problem: Zwinglianism changed under Bullinger. However, since Bullinger, in his more than forty years in office, never failed to proclaim his loyalty to his predecessor, and never uttered a word of criticism or correction, these changes were not obvious. His insistence that he was only carrying on Zwingli's work was often believed, even though that is out of the question, since it was in fact Bullinger's interpretation of Zwingli that was being carried on. It was in this form that Zwingli's influence lived on.

There is a third difficulty. The story of Zwingli's historical impact is a rather neglected area of research. There are a few summary observations of his influence on Bullinger; with regard to Calvin or other figures, there is almost a complete dearth of preliminary studies. This is true especially with regard to the seventeenth century and, for instance, Johann Jacob Breitinger, leader of the Zurich church from 1613 until 1645. In face of the broad theme, we can only give a few pointers.

2. Coming to Terms with the Defeat at Kappel

The reactions of Zwingli's friends to his death were closely linked to their overcoming the political, ecclesiastical, and spiritual crisis following the Second Kappel War. Only a second engagement, a surprise night raid by Five State volunteers on the camp of the Fortress Law cities on October 23, 1531, had sealed the military and political defeat of Zurich.

The victors had behaved with restraint during the peace negotiations that followed. The Fortress Law cities did have to dissolve all their alliances, and Zurich did have to call off its expansionist Reformation policies, but the existing confessional situation was allowed to continue in the Common Lordships. In practice, however, the result was a re-Catholicization of many districts.

But the principal goal of the Second Kappel Peace Treaty was to renew the old alliances among the Confederates and to reestablish the prewar situation. That is why Zurich could claim its position in the political-legal totality of the Confederation without incurring penalties. The traditional political institutions had survived the Reformation.

Present research is agreed that three factors in Zurich determined the results of the war: lack of strong leadership in political agencies; lack of military effectiveness; and tension between city and countryside that had increased to the point of having the rural population threatening to secede. The Five States had recognized these secession trends and started negotiations with ambassadors from the Zurich rural areas that same October 1531. This forced the city to accept a peace treaty that signified a break with previous Zurich policy goals. Previous efforts had been directed toward putting the whole Confederation under the influence of the Reformation, but now the reality of confessional partition had to be acknowledged.

In order to satisfy the situation in the rural areas, the government, in the so-called Kappel Letter dated December 9, 1531, pledged to accede to rural demands. These demands had started with the accusation that the war was the fault of both spiritual and secular warmongers, but particularly of pastors who had interfered in political affairs. The Council pledged that it would appoint only peace-loving pastors in the future, that it would check up on them more closely in general, and that it would deny them any political involvement.

Thus it is quite evident that "the stabilization and regaining of political unity was sought at the expense of the church and of the clergy."[4] Aside from the fact that the clergy had been discredited, this defeat increased doubts regarding the truthfulness of Zwingli's proclamation—doubts strongly fanned through Catholic pamphlets to this effect[5] and through Lutheran criticism.

In December 1531, the Council picked Bullinger—Zwingli himself had proposed him—to be Zwingli's successor. In the name of the clergy he expressly renounced all participation in Council committees, but did maintain his demand to be permitted to touch on political issues in the pulpit. Hans Ulrich Bächtold's solid book *Heinrich Bullinger Before the Council (Heinrich Bullinger vor dem Rat)* clearly presents the differences between the activities of Zwingli and those of Bullinger: the church, or rather, its representatives, could now exercise only in direct influence on the leaders of the state.

One of Bullinger's first tasks in the spiritual crisis following the Kappel caesura was to remove doubts of Zwingli's orthodoxy. Bullinger defended Zwingli as prophet and martyr. The biblical figures Zechariah, Stephen, and Jacob had also died a violent death; he who did not win certainly did not have the wrong faith.[6]

Myconius wrote in a similar vein in his Zwingli biography, published in 1532, and so did Johannes Stumpf.[7] A Zwingli image determined by apologetics was thus created which was not, however, really accepted outside of Zurich.

3. Heinrich Bullinger and John Calvin

The most important organizational change in Zurich from the time of Zwingli was an ecclesiastical consolidation through a new preaching and synodical regulation which was introduced in 1532. Bullinger used it to reestablish respect for the clergy; at the same time, it gave the government an effective tool for control. As J. W. Baker has proven in his careful study, Bullinger theologically expanded the covenant idea, which he made socio-politically productive.

Bullinger adopted Zwingli's starting points in the doctrine of predestination. He therefore spoke only of election and thus stood in opposition to Calvin's doctrine of double predestination and its explicit reference to the damnation of the lost. There were also some shifts in the doctrine of the Eucharist. Like Zwingli, Bullinger summarized his theology several times; most widely disseminated was the *Second Helvetic Confession (Confessio Helvetica posterior)* of 1566, which served as the confessional basis for the Reformed churches both within and outside the Confederation. On the whole, Zwinglianism entered a stabilizing phase during Bullinger's time. The confessional-political map of the Confederation has not changed since then, with the exception of a bit of retouching after the Thirty Years' War in the seventeenth century.

The question regarding Zwingli's impact on John Calvin (1509–1564) has not yet been really answered: the Geneva reformer's judgments on Zwingli are not consistent. Especially in his early period (before 1540–1541), Calvin criticized Zwingli's doctrine of the Eucharist and objected to the preference for Zwingli over Luther on the part of Luther's Swiss followers. The fault Calvin found with Zwingli's doctrine of the Eucharist was that he had conceived the Lord's Supper as a metaphorical event.

In 1549, however, Calvin and Bullinger succeeded in overcoming the differences between the Zurich and the Geneva conceptions of the Lord's Supper. The so-called Zurich Consensus (*Consensus Tigurinus*) declared that the Eucharist is not merely a metaphor for the spiritual meal. However, they retained their objection to Luther, insisting that the Spirit of God does not bind itself to the elements. Thus Calvin moved away from his original position, and Bullinger also abandoned Zwingli's conviction — without a word — by conceding to the sacraments the function of an external sealing of an inner, invisible work. Zwingli would have repudiated such a link between inner and outer. The Zurich Consensus brought a rapprochement between the Geneva and Zurich churches and allowed Calvin to find his place within the Swiss Reformed Church. But it also created a wider gulf between Calvinism and Lutheranism.

Calvin reacted more positively to Zwingli's doctrine of God; he was undoubtedly acquainted with the *Commentary*, from which he borrowed in his *Institutes*. There were also convergences on the following points: the doctrine of law; penance; coordination of faith and work, that is, justification and salvation — all of them themes on which Calvin agreed with Zwingli in opposition to Luther, and which have become typical marks of Reformed Protestantism.

Whether the word "dependence" can be used in all these cases is doubtful, since the parallels are not, as a rule, so typical of Zwingli that any other derivation would be out of the question. Nevertheless, Calvinism is inconceivable without the Zurich Reformation. Zwingli affected Calvinism through Bullinger and Calvin, and therefore he can be counted as one of the founders of Reformed Protestantism. Calvinism is rooted equally in Geneva and in the Swiss-Upper German Reformation movement.[8]

On the other hand, Calvin's differences from Zwingli and Zwinglianism cannot be overlooked. Calvin rejected Zwingli's 1530 treatise on providence, which makes the gulf between the two sides obvious with regard to the doctrine of predestination. But above all, Calvin had a different concept of the relationship between church and state.

As a loyal disciple of Zwingli, Bullinger advocated close cooperation between ecclesiastical and secular agencies: the Zurich Council, composed of Christians, has the right and the duty to regulate all aspects of church teaching and church life; independent ecclesiastical decision makers do not exist; the church has the duty to proclaim the gospel and knows how to preserve its freedom therein; thus church and state were not side by side, nor yet opposed to each other, but rather fulfilled two functions of the same community. This specifically Zurich concept can be taken as a particularity of Zwinglianism, which otherwise prevailed only in the regions of North and East Switzerland allied with Zurich, and in Bern. Objections were even raised in Bullinger's own camp in Zurich, but Bullinger was able to clear away Leo Jud's reservations.

Calvin, impressed by the conflicts between church and government in France and Geneva, rejected this Zwinglian notion of a state church and developed a church organization, independent of civil government, which was responsible for church discipline, for example. If one wished to give any reason at all for the fact that the influence of Geneva began to predominate over that of Zurich during the sixteenth century, it would be ecclesiology. Calvin's conception was more appropriate to the persecutions of Reformed churches.

Nowhere can one speak of a church basing itself on Zwingli outside the Confederation. Any documented influence is limited to individual people or individual elements. The most likely places that could be mentioned with regard to such aftereffects would be the Netherlands, the Palatinate, Hungary, England, and Scotland. We will not go into detail here.[9]

Although the name Zwingli was practically forgotten, the Reformed churches' consciousness of the unity and congruity of the Genevan and Zurich churches nevertheless survived. Zwingli continued to be effective in this fashion, even though his writings no longer provided any further impetus.

4. The Zwingli Image from the Sixteenth to the Twentieth Century

The confessionally-shaped Zwingli images remained essentially unchanged until the twentieth century. Naturally, the Catholics were the most condemnatory of Zwingli. As Fritz Büsser has demonstrated, the Catholic interpretation of Zwingli was guided by the polemics of people like John Fabri and John Eck. Aside from the usual arsenal of heresy charges and personal defamations, two elements stood out: the Zurich domestic and foreign policies for which Zwingli bore the responsibility and which had received their just reward in the defeat in Kappel and in the violent death of its instigator; and his quarrels with Luther, which proved the disunity of Protestants.

Only in 1950 did J. V. Pollet provide the breakthrough to an objective assessment of Zwingli with his balanced encyclopedia article "Zwinglianism" (*Zwinglianisme*), which was correctly labeled a masterpiece[10] and which is still one of the best summaries. At no time can one speak of any direct influence of Zwingli on Catholic theology. Zwingli's writings were very soon placed on the index of banned books; the Council of Trent condemned individual treatises (*On God's Providence*, for example) and designated Zwingli himself a heretic. Even today, Catholics still place greater emphasis on Zwingli's socio-political work than on his theology.

Luther never succeeded in separating Zwingli from Muentzer and Carlstadt. Since Luther regarded the Zuricher as his disciple, he rationalized their differences of opinion as due to Zwingli's personal peculiarities such as ambition and the need for recognition as well as to the Swiss national character, in which he included boorishness and love of war; he thought that Zwingli's death on the battlefield was God's judgment on his plans to bring about the Reformation by violent means. To this extent, Luther's opinion overlapped that of prevalent contemporary Catholic interpretations and contributed decisively to crystallizing this image. Luther did notice the improvement of morals under Zwingli's influence, but he thought this was the result of a moralistic religion lacking the correct proclamation; and that Zwingli, like John Oecolampadius, was a false teacher. However, Oskar Farner has proven that unequivocal testimony of sympathy and sorrow over Zwingli's fate can also be found in Luther's writings.

Even people closer to Zwingli, like Wolfgang Capito, Martin Bucer, and Joachim Vadian, were shocked by the reformer's death and blamed the Zurichers accordingly.

Kurt Guggisberg has described in detail the Zwingli image in Reformed Protestantism from the seventeenth to the twentieth century. A few main points from his presentation are highlighted here:

In contrast to the Catholic and the Lutheran Zwingli interpretations, the Reformed Orthodoxy of the seventeenth and eighteenth centuries underlined Zwingli's activity as prophet and systematician. In the service of God's plan of salvation, he had reestablished pure doctrine and cleaned from the cult all superstitious byproducts. He was furthermore identified with the biblical figures of Josiah, Moses, and Elijah. However, his theology was not studied in detail, because it was considered too philosophical and too rationalistic. Swiss Pietism concentrated to an astonishing degree on Luther and almost ignored Zwingli.

In Switzerland as elsewhere, a strong predilection for history became evident in the eighteenth century. This preoccupation with their own past produced collections of documents and Zwingli biographies that exhibited a pedagogical and patriotic tendency. The Zurich reformer was preferred to Luther because he was credited with having thought more freely and because he had found the solution most satisfactory to human reason in, for example, his doctrine of the Eucharist. Zwingli's liking for antiquity was applauded. The Reformation Jubilee of 1819 helped to spread this Zwingli image with a flood of popular portrayals. During the first decades of the newly formed Switzerland, Zwingli was celebrated as the noble Confederate, which led to a positive assessment of his political activities.

Ecclesiastical as well as theological life in Switzerland during the second half of the nineteenth century and into the twentieth century was determined by conflicts over alignment in which all sides cited Zwingli as their authority and each side interpreted him in its own way. The liberal Zwingli interpretation proved to be the most effective one. It regarded Zwingli as the hero of freedom who is closer to our time than any other reformer because of his achievements in public education, and indeed because of his efforts to improve morality. Emil Egli[11] and Walther Köhler[12] are responsible for this liberal Zwingli interpretation. They can be considered the pioneers of a scientific concern with Zwingli and the Zurich Reformation. The thesis of an organic link between antiquity and Christianity in Zwingli's thought, which is based on Köhler's extensive works about the Zurich reformer, dominated Zwingli interpretations for decades.

Opposition to Köhler came from Fritz Blanke (1900–1967). Blanke was Köhler's successor in the chair of church history and came from the school of the Luther researcher Karl Holl. He called attention to what Zwingli had in common with all of the Reformation and he underlined the biblical character of Zwingli's theology. According to Blanke, Köhler overestimated the antique and humanist elements in Zwingli.

The interpretation of Gottfried W. Locher is along the same lines: from the very beginning Zwingli was aware of his contrast to humanism; the focal point of his unified and, since 1522, almost unaltered theology is Christology, which was the basis of his doctrine on God and of his social-ethical impulses. Locher considered the enduring influence of Erasmus to be on the formal aspect of Zwingli's theology, which is why one could refer to a "humanistic-pedagogical tendency."[13]

It is to Locher's credit that he facilitated a general breakthrough for an appropriate evaluation of Zwingli's theology and its role in Reformed Protestantism.

5. Bibliography

Bächtold, Hans Ulrich. "Bullinger und die Krise der Zürcher Reformation im Jahre 1532." In Ulrich Gäbler and Erland Herkenrath, eds., *Heinrich Bullinger, 1504–1575. Gesammelte Aufsätze zum 400. Todestag*, 1: 269–89. Zürcher Beiträge zur Reformationsgeschichte 7. Zurich, 1975.

———. *Heinrich Bullinger vor dem Rat. Zur Gestaltung und Verwaltung des Zürcher Staatswesens in den Jahren 1531 bis 1575.* Zürcher Beiträge zur Reformationsgeschichte 12. Bern and Frankfurt am Main, 1982.

Baker, J. Wayne. *Heinrich Bullinger and the Covenant. The Other Reformed Tradition.* Ohio, 1980.

Berchtold-Belart, Jakob. *Das Zwinglibild und die zürcherischen Reformationschroniken. Eine textkritische Untersuchung.* Quellen und Abhandlungen zur schweizerischen Reformationsgeschichte 5. Leipzig, 1929.

Blanke, Fritz. "Calvins Urteile über Zwingli." *Zwingliana* 11 (1959): 66–92. Reprint in *Aus der Welt der Reformation*, 18–47. Zurich and Stuttgart, 1960.

Büsser, Fritz. *Das katholische Zwinglibild. Von der Reformation bis zur Gegenwart.* Zurich and Stuttgart, 1968.

———. "De prophetae officio. Eine Gedenkrede Bullingers auf Zwingli." In *Festgabe Leonhard von Muralt. Zum 70. Geburtstag*, 245–57. Zurich, 1970.

———. "Bullinger, Heinrich." In *Theologische Realenzyklopädie*, 7: 375–87. Berlin and New York, 1981.

Courvoisier, Jaques. "Zwingli et Karl Barth." In *Antwort. Karl Barth zum 70. Geburtstag*, 369–87. Zollikon and Zurich, 1956.

Erichson, Alfred. *Zwinglis Tod und dessen Beurteilung durch Zeitgenossen.* Strasbourg, 1883.

Farner, Oskar. *Das Zwinglibild Luthers.* Sammlung gemeinverständlicher Vorträge und Schriften aus dem Gebiete der Theologie und Religionsgeschichte 151. Tübingen, 1931.

Ficker, Johannes. "Verzeichnisse von Schriften Zwinglis auf gegnerischer Seite." *Zwingliana* 5 (1930): 152–75.

Freudenberger, Theobald. "Zur Benützung des reformatorischen Schrifttums im Konzil von Trient." In Remigius Bäumer, ed., *Von Konstanz nach Trient. Beiträge zur Geschichte der Kirche von den Reformkonzilien bis zum Tridentinum. Festgabe für August Franzen*, 577–601. Munich, Paderborn, and Vienna, 1972.

Gäbler, Ulrich. "Consensus Tigurinus." In *Theologische Realenzyklopädie*, 8: 189–92. Berlin and New York, 1981.

———. "Heinrich Bullinger." In Martin Greschat, ed., *Gestalten der Kirchengeschichte*, 6: 197–209. Stuttgart, Berlin, Cologne, and Mainz, 1981.

Guggisberg, Kurt. *Das Zwinglibild des Protestantismus im Wandel der Zeiten.* Quellen und Abhandlungen zur schweizerischen Reformationsgeschichte 8. Leipzig, 1934.

Hauri, Rudolf. *Die Reformation in der Schweiz im Urteil der neueren schweizerischen Geschichtsschreibung.* Schweizer Studien zur Geschichtswissenschaft, Neue Folge 7. Zurich, 1945.

Hauswirth, René. "Zur politischen Ethik der Generation nach Zwingli." *Zwingliana* 13 (1971): 305–42.

———. "Stabilisierung als Aufgabe der politischen und kirchlichen Führung in Zürich nach der Katastrophe von Kappel." In Bernd Moeller, ed., *Stadt und Kirche im 16. Jahrhundert.* Schriften des Vereins für Reformationsgeschichte 190. Gütersloh, 1978.

Humbel, Frida. *Ulrich Zwingli und seine Reformation im Spiegel der gleichzeitigen, schweizerischen volkstümlichen Literatur.* Quellen und Abhandlungen zur schweizerischen Reformationsgeschichte 1. Leipzig, 1912.

Koch, Ernst. "Zwingli, Calvin und der Calvinismus im Geschichtsbild des Marxismus." *Zwingliana* 14 (1974/75): 61–88.

Köhler, Walter. "Zwingli und Schleiermacher." *Zwingliana* 4 (1922): 92–93.

Kressner, Helmut. *Schweizer Ursprünge des anglikanischen Staatskirchentums.* Schriften des Vereins für Reformationsgeschichte 170. Gütersloh, 1953.

Maeder, Kurt. "Die Unruhe der Zürcher Landschaft nach Kappel (1531/32) oder: Aspekte einer Herrschaftskrise." *Zwingliana* 14 (1974/1975): 109–44.

Meyer, Helmut. *Der Zweite Kappeler Krieg. Die Krise der Schweizerischen Reformation.* Zurich, 1976.

Muralt, Leonhard von. "Von Zwingli zu Pestalozzi." *Zwingliana* 9 (1951): 329–64.

Pestalozzi, Carl. *Heinrich Bullinger, Leben und ausgewählte Schriften. Nach handschriftlichen und gleichzeitigen Quellen.* Leben und ausgewählte Schriften der Väter und Begründer der reformierten Kirche 6. Elberfeld, 1858.

Pollet, Jacques Vincent. "Zwinglianisme." In *Dictionnaire de Théologie catholique,* 15: 3745–3828. Paris, 1950.

———. *Huldrych Zwingli et la Réforme en Suisse d'après les recherches récentes.* Paris, 1963.

Schmidt-Clausing, Fritz. "Das Zwingli-Bild Leopold von Rankes." *Zwingliana* 14 (1974/1975): 145–53.

Senn, Matthias. "Alltag und Lebensgefühl im Zürich des 16. Jahrhunderts." *Zwingliana* 14 (1976): 251–62.

Staedtke, Joachim. "Der Zürcher Prädestinationsstreit von 1560." *Zwingliana* 9 (1953): 536–46.

———. "Bullingers Theologie—eine Fortsetzung der zwinglischen?" In Ulrich Gäbler and Endre Zsindely, eds., *Bullinger-Tagung 1975. Vorträge, gehalten aus Anlass von Heinrich Bullingers 400. Todestag,* 87–98. Zurich, 1977; Reprint, 1982.

Walton, Robert C. "The Institutionalization of the Reformation at Zurich." *Zwingliana* 13 (1972): 497–515.

XI

BIBLIOGRAPHICAL SURVEY

1. Bibliographies

Two bibliographies offer satisfactory access to Zwingli material: Georg Finsler, *Zwingli-Bibliographie. Verzeichnis der gedruckten Schriften von und über Ulrich Zwingli* (Zurich, 1897; reprint, Nieuwkoop, 1962, 1968), lists the publications until 1896, supplemented by Ulrich Gäbler, *Huldrych Zwingli im 20. Jahrhundert. Forschungsbericht und annotierte Bibliographie, 1897–1972* (Zurich, 1975). The periodical *Zwingliana* reports annually the important publications since that date. Research from various points of view are treated in Jacques Vincent Pollet, *Huldrych Zwingli et la Réforme en Suisse d'après les recherches récentes* (Paris, 1963); Gottfried W. Locher, "Die Wandlung des Zwingli-Bildes in der neueren Forschung," in Gottfried W. Locher, ed., *Huldrych Zwingli in neuer Sicht. Zehn Beiträge zur Theologie der Zürcher Reformation* (Stuttgart and Zurich, 1969), 137–71; and Gäbler, *Zwingli im 20. Jahrhundert*, 11–102.

2. Collections of Sources on the Zurich Reformation

Edited treatments of archival sources regarding Zwingli's activities are contained in the collection *Die Eidgenössischen Abschiede;* of particular importance are vol. III/2, *1500–1520,* ed. Anton Philipp Segesser (Lucerne, 1869); vol. IV/1a, *1521–1528,* ed. Johannes Strickler (Brugg, 1873); vol. IV/1b, *1529–1532,* ed. Johannes Strickler

(Zurich, 1876). They contain the decrees of the Diets, often accompanied by supplementary records like reports of Confederate officials, ambassadorial instructions, letters, and information from foreign powers. Records of church historical importance are contained in *Actensammlung zur Schweizerischen Reformationsgeschichte in den Jahren 1521-1532*, appended to the contemporary Confederate resolutions, edited by Johannes Strickler; 5 volumes (Zurich, 1878-1884). In addition, Basel, Bern, and Zurich have collections of their own. *Actensammlung zur Geschichte der Zürcher Reformation in den Jahren 1519-1533*, ed. Emil Egli (Zurich, 1879; reprint, Aalen, 1973; Nieuwkoop, 1973; abridged, *Actensammlung*) is essential to any treatment of sources concerning Zwingli, even though this edition is out of date, contains errors, and does not have enough indexes. Complementary source items are given in Emil Egli, *Analecta Reformatoria I. Dokumente und Abhandlungen zur Geschichte Zwinglis und seiner Zeit* (Zurich, 1899).

3. Editions of Zwingli's Works

After Zwingli's death, when there were renewed efforts to achieve concord between the Protestant religious parties, Zwingli's understanding of the Eucharist was maintained, but was defamed as heretical by the opposition. In order to confront this charge, his letters and those of John Oecolampadius were published in Basel in 1536: *Ioannis Oecolampadii et Huldrichi Zwinglii epistolarum libri quatuor, 1536*. Many of the letters printed in this collection were later lost or were destroyed immediately after being set in type. A short time afterward, a "complete edition" of Zwingli's works in Latin appeared, which again points to the fact that the Zurich publisher Rudolf Gwalther wanted to reach the well-educated in particular. This edition reproduced the Latin texts in the original wording and the German text was a translation by Gwalther himself. It remained the definitive text for the study of Zwingli's works for a long time. Only in the nineteenth century was it superseded by the edition of Melchior Schuler and Johannes Schulthess (Zurich 1828-1842; Supplement, 1861) in eight volumes; it has become customary to use the symbol S as an abbreviation. This outdated edition must still be used for all exegetical writings and for works dated after November 1530.

For other items, the critical edition within the *Corpus Reformatorum* (vols. 88–101) offers the most dependable reprint: *Huldreich Zwinglis sämtliche Werke*, edited by Emil Egli, Georg Finsler, Walther Köhler, Oskar Farner, Fritz Blane, Leonhard von Muralt, Edwin Künzli, Joachim Staedtke, Fritz Büsser, with the participation of the Zwingli Society in Zurich. This edition has been appearing since 1905, and is available in reprint. It is usually denoted with the symbol Z, and is divided into four sections: volumes Z I to Z VI/III encompass Zwingli's writings up to November 1530 in chronological order; volume Z VI/IV is still missing. The second section, Z VII to XI, contains the correspondence (with indexes of names and places in vol. XI). The twelfth volume contains book entries and is not yet completed. Of Zwingli's exegetical works, two volumes of Old Testament interpretations have appeared: Z XIII contains the commentaries on Genesis and Exodus, the translations of Job and Psalms, and the commentary on Psalm passages. The commentaries on the Prophets are published in vol. XIV.

Still unsettled is the new edition of New Testament exegetical writings (printed in S VI/I and VI/II) as well as copies of sermons. The printed text of translated excerpts from these sources, contained in the collections *Aus Zwinglis Predigten zu Jesaja und Jeremia. Unbekannte Nachschriften*, selected and linguistically edited by Oskar Farner (Zurich, 1957), and *Aus Zwinglis Predigten zu Matthäus, Markus und Johannes*, selected and translated by Oskar Farner (Zurich, 1957), is in many ways so far removed from the original that it is scientifically worthless. Finally, we are still lacking an edition of the songs of Zwingli, but see Markus Jenny, "Die Lieder Zwinglis," *Jahrbuch für Liturgik und Hymnologie* 14 (1969): 63–102.

A serious deficiency is the lack of indexes to the critical edition. Nor does an anthology of writings and letters in the original language exist. There is not much hope of having these gaps filled in the foreseeable future.

The most important collection, the series *Zwingli Hauptschriften*, edited by Fritz Blanke, Oskar Farner, Oskar Frei, and Rudolf Pfister (Zurich, 1940–   ), presents the German works in the original language and the Latin in German translation. It too has remained a mere torso. The eight volumes are divided into the following parts:

The Preacher (vols. 1 and 2) contains particularly writings based on sermons; *Defender of the Faith* (vols. 3 and 4) contains the *Concluding Statements; The Statesman* (vol. 7) has, among other things, the treatise *On Divine and Human Righteousness (Von göttlicher und menschlicher Gerechtigkeit);* and finally, *The Theologian* (vols. 9–11) contains a translation of the *Commentary* and of the two confessions *Account of Faith (Ratio fidei)* and *Exposition of Faith (Expositio fidei)* abbreviated with the symbol *HS.*

The best one-volume collection of Zwingli works is *Huldrych Zwingli. Auswahl seiner Schriften,* ed. Edwin Künzli (Zurich and Stuttgart, 1962). Very few of Zwingli's works have appeared in single-volume editions. Fifty of his letters are in the volume *Reformatorenbriefe,* ed. Günther Gloede (East Berlin, 1973).

An excellent introduction to Zwingli texts is offered by *Huldrych Zwingli. An den jungen Mann. Zwinglis Erziehungsschrift aus dem Jahre 1523,* newly edited by Ernst Gerhard Rüsch (Zwingli Bücherei 62, Zurich, 1957); and *Huldrych Zwingli. Christliche Anleitung,* translated into modern German and edited by Gerhard G. Muras (Furche-Bücherei 207, Hamburg, 1962; 2d ed., Gütersloher Taschenbuch 264, Gütersloh, 1977); or the apt paraphrases of Zwingli's most important works in August Bauer, *Zwinglis Theologie. Ihr Werden und ihr System,* 2 vols. (Halle, 1885–1889); and Paul Wernle, *Der evangelische Glaube nach den Hauptschriften der Reformatoren,* vol. II; *Zwingli* (Tübingen, 1919).

These English editions are outstanding among the foreign language editions: *The Latin Works of Huldreich Zwingli,* ed. Samuel Maccauley Jackson, William John Hinke, and Clarence Nevin Heller (New York, London, Philadelphia, 1912, 1922, 1929). Three volumes have appeared so far. Almost totally dedicated to Zwingli is the edition *Zwingli and Bullinger. Selected Translations with Introductions and Notes,* ed. G. W. Bromiley (The Library of Christian Classics 24, London, 1953). A reprint appeared in Philadelphia in 1979. The only useful index of Zwingli works with indications of where they can be found in the various editions has unfortunately appeared in a difficult work to find: Minoru Uchiyama, "Manuale zum Zwinglistudium," *Studies in Humanities and Social Sciences* 17 (Tokyo, 1975): 211–44.

4. General Portrayals

The basis for all the older descriptions of Zwingli's life is the biography written in 1532 by his friend Oswald Myconius, *De domini Huldrichi Zuinglii fortissimi herois ac theologi doctissimi vita et obitu*, published under the title *Vom Leben und Sterben Huldrych Zwinglis* in a bilingual edition by Ernst Gerhard Rüsch (Mitteilungen zur vaterländischen Geschichte 50, St. Gallen, 1979). This biography preceded the edition of the letters of 1536 mentioned above, and was intended as a defense of the reformer's orthodox faith as well as of his political activities; references to any negative traits are of course hard to find.

Zwingli's successor Heinrich Bullinger described the whole Zurich reformation, but his work was not published until the nineteenth century: *Einrich Bullingers Reformationsgeschichte*, 3 vols., transcribed from the handwritten manuscript at the request of the "Vaterländisch-historischen Gesellschaft" in Zurich by J. J. Hottinger and H. H. Vögeli (Frauenfeld, 1838, 1840), with an index by Willy Wuhrmann (Zurich, 1913). Bullinger stressed the independence of the Zurich Reformation in relation to Lutheranism, which reflects Bullinger's theological self-confidence. Since the author frequently referred to original sources and quoted them literally, his work remains valuable. His portrayal of Zwingli's work is guided by veneration for his great predecessor, and forms the basis for an emphatically "Zurich" viewpoint.

Leopold von Ranke was the first to break with the preferential treatment given the local-historical aspect, and to tie the Zurich Reformation in with general history. Gottfried W. Locher is at the end of this historiographical line, with *Die Zwinglische Reformation im Rahmen der europäischen Kirchengeschichte* (Göttingen and Zurich, 1979), and the title immediately makes the trend in his presentation obvious. Among the biographies of our century, an impressive one is Walther Köhler, *Huldrych Zwingli* (Leipzig, 1943; rev. ed., Stuttgart, 1952 and Leipzig, 1954). He was the first to successfully overcome the problem of a Zwingli biography referred to above, and to allow the reformer "to come alive in the inseparable interwovenness of politics and religion."[1] However, the book is outdated today, both in its general conception (Zwingli's world of ideas as synthesis of antiquity and Christianity) and on individual points (such as the determination of Zwingli's share in political decisions), and it is less useful for further research because of its lack of documentation.

The strength of the four-volume biography by Oskar Farner[2] is its exhaustive use of biographical material from Zwingli's writings. But it suffers from imbalance (the period up to 1519 takes up one-half of the work), which can be traced back to the fact that Farner could not — because of his age — carry out his original, more extensive plan. Moreover, the apologetical tendency permeating the whole work lessens its value significantly.

Against the background of a broad description of Zwingli's political, social, and economic environment, Martin Haas paints a striking portrait of Zwingli's life in *Huldrych Zwingli und seine Zeit* (Zurich, 1969; 3d ed. 1982), in which the theological aspects lose importance. Fritz Schmidt-Clausing pays more attention to Zwingli's theology in *Zwingli* (Sammlung Göschen 1219, Berlin, 1965; Italian ed., Turin, 1978), but the facts are distorted through his occasional overemphases.

The brief description of Zwingli's life by Fritz Büsser, *Huldrych Zwingli. Reformation als prophetischer Auftrag* (Persönlichkeit und Geschichte 74/75, Göttingen, 1973) is an excellent introduction.

To a certain extent a summary and provisional ending to Zwingli biographies is the above-mentioned magisterial work by Locher, who consistently portrays Zwingli as the illustration of Middle European history. On the whole, it is in fact less a Zwingli portrayal than a description of the history and impact of the Zurich Reformation. For the first time, an effort is made to organize and describe this diffuse material, the boundaries of which simply cannot be methodologically established with any certainty. The author's own, sometimes highly individual, viewpoint lends color to his presentation, but carries the danger that readers will receive an inadequate impression of the complexity of the problems and the temporariness of the solutions presented. Locher also published a summary in the series *Die Kirche in ihrer Geschichte*, entitled *Zwingli und die schweizerische Reformation* (vol. 3, Lieferung J 1, Göttingen, 1982) which includes the most recent literature and contains modified answers to several questions. Locher's most important essays on Zwingli's theology are contained in *Huldrych Zwingli in neuer Sicht. Zehn Beiträge zur Theologie der Zürcher Reformation* (Zurich and Stuttgart, 1969), expanded by five contributions and translated into English as *Zwingli's Thought. New Perspectives* (Studies in the History of Christian Thought 25, Leiden, 1981).

Strangely enough, there are no modern, broadly executed, scientifically based descriptions of Zwingli's life in German like these two solid works: George Richard Potter, *Zwingli* (Cambridge, 1976) and Francesco Erasmo Sciuto, *Ulrico Zwingli. La vita – il pensiero – il suo tempo* (Geminae ortae 9, Naples, 1980). Narrower goals are pursued in the biographies by Jean Rilliet, *Zwingli. Le troisième homme de la Réforme* (Paris, 1959; in English: London, 1964) and Klaas Maarten Witteween, *Het Evangelie tussen pacifisme en geweld. Huldrych Zwingli* (Kampen, 1974).

No monograph of the history of the Swiss Reformation exists. Still essential for the period up to 1525 is Emil Egli, *Schweizerische Reformationsgeschichte*, vol. I: *Umfassend die Jahre 1519–1525*, published on commission of the Zwingli Society in Zurich by Georg Finsler (Zurich, 1910). Nothing more was published.

The best survey of Swiss history and church history is presented in *Handbuch der Schweizer Geschichte*, 2 vols. (Zurich, 1972, 1977) as well as in Rudolf Pfister, *Kirchengeschichte der Schweiz*, 2 vols. (Zurich, 1964, 1974); a third and final volume is expected in the foreseeable future.

XII

ZWINGLI CHRONOLOGY

1484	January 1: Zwingli born in Wildhaus (Toggenburg).
1489–1498	Schooling in Weesen, Basel, Bern.
1498–1506	University studies in Vienna and Basel.
1506	Pastorate in Glarus.
1510	*The Poetic Fable About the Ox.*
1513	Accompanied Glarus Troops to Novarra.
1514–1516	*The Labyrinth.*
1515	Accompanied Glarus troops to Marignano.
1516	Visited Erasmus in Basel; November: Pastorate in Einsiedeln.
1519	January 1: Became people's priest at Zurich Great Minster; became ill with the plague.
1521	April 29: Promoted to Canon.
1522	March 9: "Sausage Meal" at the home of Christoph Frowschauer; April 7–9: Disputation with episcopal delegation; April 16: *Regarding the Choice and the Freedom of Food;* July 21: Disputation with mendicant monks; August 22–23: *The First and Last Word;* September 6: *Regarding Clarity and Certainty of the Word of God;*

175

September 17: *A Sermon About the Eternally Pure Maid Mary.*

1523   January 29: First Zurich Disputation;

July 14: *Analysis and Reasons for the Concluding Statements;*

July 30: *Regarding Divine and Human Righteousness;*

August 1: *Little Textbook;*

September 29: New regulations for the Great Minster;

October 26–28: Second Zurich Disputation;

November 17: *Short Christian Introduction.*

1524   January 13–14: Disputation with traditional canons;

April 2: Marriage to Anna Reinhart;

April 8: Alliance of the Five States in Defense against the Reformation;

June: Removal of pictures and statues from Zurich churches;

October 24: Dissolution of the Mary Minster;

November: *Letter to Matthew Alber Regarding the Lord's Supper;*

December 28: *Whoever Causes Unrest.*

1525   January 15: Welfare laws;

January 17: Disputation with opponents of infant baptism;

January 21: First adult baptism;

March: *Commentary About the True and False Religion;*

March 26: *The Shepherd;*

March–April: *Act or Custom of the Supper;*

April: Appointed school supervisor;

April 13: Revision of the Eucharist celebration;

May 10: Marriage laws;

May 27: *On Baptism, Anabaptism, and Infant Baptism;*

June 19: "Prophecy" opens;

August: Council mandate for political and economic reorganization.

1526   February: *A Clear Briefing About Christ's Supper;*

May 19–June 9: Baden Disputation.

1527   July 31: *Refutation of the Schemes of the Anabaptists;*

December: Fortress Law alliance of Zurich with Constance.

1528 Fortress Law alliance of Zurich with Bern and St. Gallen;
      Zurich church regulations;
      January 6–26: Bern Disputation;
      February 7: Reformation laws in Bern;
      April 21: First Synod in Zurich.

1529 Fortress Law alliance of Zurich with Basel, Schaffhausen,
      Biel, and Mulhausen;
      April: Reformation laws in Basel;
      April 22: "Christian Union" of Five States with Ferdinand I;
      June 26: First Kappel Peace Treaty;
      September: Reformation laws in Schaffhausen;
      October 1–4: Marburg Colloquy.

1530 July 3: *Account of Faith*
      August 20: *Remembrance of the Sermon About God's
      Providence;*
      November: Alliance between Zurich and Hesse.

1531 May: Food blockage against the Five States;
      July: Zwingli offered to resign; *Exposition of the Christian
      Faith;*
      October 11: Battle at Kappel and Zwingli's death.

NOTES

Chapter I. The Environment

1. Emil Egli, *Schweizerische Reformationsgeschichte* (Zurich, 1910), I:6.
2. *Huldrych Zwingli sämtliche Werke*, ed. Emil Egli et al., I:270:25–27 (hereafter cited as Z).
3. Z IV:48:15–49:6; XII:151:35.
4. Rudolf Brun died in 1360.
5. From *constabularii* meaning "cavalry"; thus citizens who could do their military service on horseback.
6. Z VI/II:639:13; X:43:2–4.
7. Leonhard von Muralt, "Zum Problem der Theokratie bei Zwingli," in *Discordia Concors* (Basel and Stuttgart, 1968), 2:379.
8. Otto Sigg, "Bevölkerungs-, agrar-, und sozialgeschichtliche Probleme des 16. Jahrhunderts am Beispiel der Zürcher Landschaft," *Schweizerische Zeitschrift für Geschichte* 24 (1974): 2.
9. Oskar Vasella, *Reform und Reformation in der Schweiz, Zur Würdigung der Anfänge der Glaubenskrise*, 2d ed. (Münster, 1965).

Chapter II. Childhood and Student Years

1. *Concluding Statements, Commentarius, Fidei Ratio, De Providentia Dei, Expositio Fidei.*
2. Z III:486:3.
3. J. V. Pollet, *Huldrych Zwingli et la Réforme en Suisse d'après les Recherches récentes* (Paris, 1963), 14–15.

Chapter III. Pastorate in Glarus and Einsiedeln (1506–1518)

1. Z I:1–22.
2. Z I:23–37.

3. Joachim Rogge, *Zwingli und Erasmus. Die Friedensgedanken des jungen Zwingli* (Berlin, 1962), 20.

4. Z I:39–60.

5. Z VII:337:10.

6. Z V:714:2–3.

7. Z VII:31; I:38.

8. Z VII:68–71, October 30, 1517.

9. *Actensammlung zur Schweizerischen Reformationsgeschichte in den Jahren 1521–1532*, ed. Johannes Strickler (Zurich, 1834).

10. Venice, 1503.

11. Z XII:1–400.

12. Z VI/II:150:13.

13. J. F. Gerhard Goeters, "Zwinglis Werdegang als Erasmianer," in *Reformation und Humanismus, Robert Strupperich zum 65. Geburtstag* (Witten, 1969), 23–24.

14. Ibid., 261.

15. Z VII:22:12. Letter to Joachim Vadian, February 22, 1513.

16. Z VII:35–36. This letter, as well as Erasmus's reply, is not dated; a possible date could also be spring of 1515.

17. Joachim Rogge, "Die Initia Zwinglis und Luthers. Eine Einführung in die Probleme," *Luther-Jahrbuch* 30 (1963): 129.

Chapter IV. Awakening in Zurich (1519–1522)

1. Z VII:110–13.

2. See Farner, *Zwingli* III, 35.

3. Paul Wernle, Walther Köhler, Oskar Farner.

4. Cornelius Augustijn.

5. See below, p. 108.

6. Z V:712:24–715:1.

7. Letter to Beatus Rhenanus, June 7, 1519. Z VII:181:7.

8. Farner, *Zwingli* III, 31.

9. Utinger's key role at the Great Minster, and in the history of the Zurich Reformation in general, has not yet been investigated thoroughly. He died in 1536.

10. March 9, 1522.

11. Z II:778:11.

12. Z I:74–136. Jackson, I:70–112.

13. Z I:99:14–15.

14. Z I:106:15–17.

15. Z I:125:31–32.

16. Z I:109:2–4.

17. Z I:136:1–7.

18. Z I:137–54.

19. *Actensammlung*, 236.

20. J. F. Gerhard Goeters, "Die Vorgeschichte des Täufertums in Zurich,"

in *Studien zur Geschichte und Theologie der Reformation* (Neukirchen, 1969), 243.

21. July 30, 1522, to Beatus Rhenanus. Z VII:549:3–5.

22. *Supplicatio ad Hugonem episcopum Constantiensem (Petition to the Constance Bishop Hugo).* Z I:189–209.

23. *Eine freundliche Bitte und Ermahnung an die Eidgenossen.* July 13, 1522. Z I:210–48.

24. Died in 1538.

25. Z I:249–327.

26. Z VII:582. September 8, 1522, to Zwingli.

27. Locher, *Zwingli,* 1982, 22.

28. See Robert C. Walton, *Zwingli's Theocracy* (Toronto, 1967), 131; Bernd Moeller, "Zwinglis Disputationen. Studien zu den Anfängen der Kirchenbildung und des Synodal Wesens im Protestantismus," *Zeitschrift der Savigny-Stiftung für Rechtsgeschichte* 87 (1970): I:293; 91 (1974): II:215.

29. P. 274.

30. September 6, 1522. Z I:328–84.

31. Z I:352:7.

32. September 17, 1522. Z I:385–428.

33. Z I:426:22–23.

Chapter V. Breakthrough in Zurich (1523–1525)

1. May 16, 1522. Z I:155:88.

2. November 1522. Z I:429–41.

3. Z I:466–68.

4. For instance Z I:246:26–247:3; 324:29–30; 466:21–22.

5. Theodor Pestalozzi, *Die Gegner Zwinglis am Grossmünsterstift in Zürich* (Zurich, 1918), 56:85.

6. Z I:458–65.

7. As claimed by Emil Egli, *Schweizer Reformationsgeschichte* (Zurich, 1910), 79; Walther Köhler, *Huldrych Zwingli* (Leipzig, 1943; rev. ed. Stuttgart, 1952; Leipzig, 1954), 93; Farner, *Zwingli* III, 337.

8. Z I 458:5.

9. Z I:458:11–12; First Concluding Statement.

10. Z I:458:13–17. Second and Third Concluding Statements.

11. Thirteenth Concluding Statement.

12. Fifteenth Concluding Statement.

13. Sixteenth Concluding Statement.

14. Gottfried W. Locher, "Grundzüge der Theologie Huldrych Zwinglis im Vergleich mit derjenigen Martin Luthers und Johannes Calvins," in *Huldrych Zwingli in neuer Sicht* (Zurich and Stuttgart, 1969), 269.

15. Forty-second Concluding Statement.

16. Heiko Augustinus Oberman, *Werden und Wertung der Reformation* (Tübingen, 1977), 245 n. 11.

17. See Z I:472–569. Other sources are mentioned by Moeller, "Zwinglis Disputationen," I:279–81.

18. Oberman, *Werden und Wertung*, 290.

19. Z I:469–71.

20. Z I:470:6–7.

21. E.g., Steven E. Ozment, *The Reformation in the Cities* (New Haven and London, 1975), 125, 136.

22. Above all Moeller, "Zwinglis Disputationen," stressed by Oberman, *Werden und Wertung*, 284.

23. Moeller, "Zwinglis Disputationen," 1:319; Egli asserted this in *Schweizerische Reformationsgeschichte*, 77, and in Z I:443.

24. Farner, *Zwingli* III, 332.

25. Oberman, *Werden und Wertung*, 248.

26. Ibid., 249.

27. Ibid., 292.

28. July 31, 1523, to Wattenwyl. Z VIII:102:15–19.

29. Moeller, "Zwinglis Disputationen," I:321.

30. July 14, 1523. Z II:1–457.

31. Z II:252:11–12.

32. Z II:201:10.

33. E.g., Z II:267:22.

34. Z II:452:7–15.

35. Z II:170:11–26.

36. Z II:283:21–25; 186:16–20.

37. E.g., Z II:23:6–9; 392:20–393:2.

38. Z II:45:9–34.

39. Z II:148:3–30; 380:16–20.

40. Z II:144:17–150:26.

41. Congregation (*Gemeinde*) or *kirchhöri*. Z II:55:32–61:21.

42. Z II:310:13–16.

43. Z II:327:23–26.

44. S I/I:553.

45. July 30, 1523. Z II:458–525.

46. Z II:490:10–12.

47. Leonhard von Muralt.

48. Gottfried W. Locher, *Die Zwinglische Reformation im Rahmen der europäischen Kirchengeschichte* (Göttingen and Zurich, 1979), 618–19.

49. Ozment, *Reformation in the Cities*, 131–38.

50. Christof Gestrich, *Zwingli als Theologe. Glaube und Geist beim Zürcher Reformator* (Zurich and Stuttgart, 1967), 176.

51. August 29, 1523. Z II:552–608.

52. October 9, 1523. Z II:617–25.

53. Printed, Z II 678:18–680:4. The sources contradict each other regarding the form of the announcement. Invitations to various people were probably sent on different days.

54. Z VIII:103:6–104:26. July 31, 1523, to Nicholaus von Wattenwyl.
55. Z II:666.
56. Z II:664–803.
57. Z II 697:15–16; 698:6.
58. Locher, Zwingli, 1982, 64.
59. Z II:784:12–13.
60. Z II:784:14–16.
61. Z II:784:26.
62. Z II:794:7–796:30.
63. Z II:796:1–5.
64. Z II:796:13–14.
65. E.g., in Köhler, Huldrych Zwingli, 111.
66. November 17, 1523. Z II:626–63.
67. August Baur, Zwinglis Theologie. Ihr Werden und ihr System (Halle, 1885), 1:344.
68. Z II:654:63.
69. Ibid.
70. Z II:646–53.
71. Z II:649:24.
72. Z II:651:19–20.
73. J. F. Gerhard Goeters, "Die Vorgeschichte des Täufertums in Zurich," in Studien zur Geschichte und Theologie der Reformation (Neukirchen, 1969), 265.
74. The Shepherd (Der Hirt); see pp. 86–87.
75. May 1524. Z:III:114–31.
76. Actensammlung, 489.
77. Z III:146–47.
78. August 18, 1524. Z III:146–229.
79. Annotation to 'The Three Bishops' Presentation to the Confederates (Anmerkungen zu: 'der drei Bischöfe Vortrag an die Eidgenossen'). April 1524. Z III:69–85.
80. A Loyal and Sincere Admonition to the Confederate States (Eine treue und ernstliche Vermahnung an die Eidgenossen) May 2, 1524. Z III:97–113.
81. Z III:511–38.
82. December 1524. Z III:355–469.
83. August 20, 1524. Z III:230–87.
84. March 1525. Z III:628–912.
85. March 26, 1524. Z III:1–68.
86. Z III:12–45, 45–65.
87. Z III:63:24–64:11.
88. E.g., Z III:888:26; 907:5–16.
89. Z III:723:5–6.
90. Z III:629:16–18.
91. Z III:757:20–23; translated by Fritz Blanke, HS 10:27–28.
92. Z III:74:4–32.

93. Z III:909:27–28.
94. E.g., Z III:705:7–15; 723:1–5.
95. Z III:705:16–33.
96. Z III:844:25–32.
97. Z III:867–88.
98. Z III:773–820.
99. Z III:867:12–13.

Chapter VI. Church Organization (1524–1526)

1. James M. Stayer, "Die Anfänge des schweizerischen Täufertums im reformierten Kongregationalismus," in Hans-Jürgen Goertz, ed., *Umstrittenes Täufertum, 1525–1975*, 2d ed. (Göttingen, 1977), 30.
2. December 28, 1524. Z III:355–469.
3. Z III:399:24–27.
4. Z III:454:6–8; see also Z III:449:22 and 459:15–17.
5. Z III:462:16.
6. Z III:446:13–14.
7. Z III:446:33–447:4; 462:12–14; 466:15–29.
8. Z IV:338–60.
9. Z IV:530–45.
10. Z III:457:24–458:1; 463:21–23.
11. Z III:503–10.
12. *Actensammlung*, 619.
13. Christian Reputation (*Das christliche Ansehen*). *Actensammlung*, 426.
14. Originally Latin, *Quo pacto ingenui adolescentes formandi sint.* Z II:526–51; published by him in 1526 in German, Z V:426–47.
15. Z VII:345:14–16. July 24, 1520, to Oswald Myconius.
16. Z IV:701:6; IV:393:26–419:6.
17. See Z IV:361–65.
18. Reprint. Z IV:365:1–6.
19. Farner, *Zwingli* III, 558–59.
20. Walter Meyer, "Die Entstehung von Huldrych Zwinglis neutestamentlichen Kommentaren und Predigtnachschriften," *Zwingliana* 13 (1976): 330–31.
21. Printed. Z XIII and XIV.
22. Z VI/II:283–312.
23. Z IV:176, 187.
24. *Actensammlung*, 1664.
25. Ibid., 944.
26. Z III:807:25–808:11.
27. Compare Z IV:25–30.
28. Z III:129:4–15.

29. March/April 1525. Z IV:1–24.
30. This is Locher's assertion, in *Zwinglische Reformation*, 146.
31. Markus Jenny, *Die Einheit des Abendmahlsgottesdienstes bei den elsässischen und schweizerischen Reformatoren* (Zurich and Stuttgart, 1968), 67–68.
32. May 27, 1525. Z IV:188–337, esp. 334–37.
33. Z IV:671–94.
34. Jenny, *Einheit des Abendmahlsgottesdienstes*, 38–39.
35. April 27, 1525. Z IV:35–159.
36. Z I:62–69.
37. Markus Jenny, "Die Lieder Zwinglis," *Jahrbuch für Liturgik und Hymnologie* 14 (1969): 73.

Chapter VII. Reformation in the Confederation (1524–1529)

1. *Answer to John Eck's Missive and Offer (Antwort auf Johannes Ecks Missiv und Enbieten)*, August 31, 1524. Z III:288–312.
2. Z III:309:12–13.
3. Z III:299.
4. Z V:179:4–13; 215:5–14.
5. Z V:171–95; 207–36.
6. Locher, *Zwinglische Reformation*, 186.
7. E.g., on August 19, 1530, in *Supplication and Desire of the Preachers in Zurich (Supplikation und Begehren der Prädikanten zu Zürich)*. Z VI/II:832–43.
8. The inferred German name *Hüssgen* was interpreted as *Hausschein* (house brilliance) and transposed into the appropriate Greek.
9. Walther Köhler, "Zwingli und Basel," *Zwingliana* 5 (1929): 6.
10. November 19, 1527, Haller to Zwingli. Z IX:309:19–21.
11. Z VI/I:243:10–244:9.
12. See Z VI/I:213–17; 233–42; 563–65.
13. Z VI/I:243–432.
14. Z VI/I:499–508.
15. E.g., Leonhard von Muralt, Z VI/I:502.
16. Z VI/I:498:31.
17. Z VI/I:443–92.
18. Z VI/I:450:4.
19. Z VI/I:453:1.
20. Z VI/I:455:1.
21. Z VI/I:463:24–28.
22. Z VI/I:469–88.
23. Z VI/I:493–99.
24. Compare Z IX:457:24–458:3. May 4, 1528 to Ambrosius Blarer.
25. Z III:539–83. Z dates the piece too early.
26. End of May 1529. Z VI/II:424–40.

27. See Locher, *Zwinglische Reformation*, 328. He considers the statement by Canon Hans Edlibach unreliable.

Chapter VIII. Conflict About the Sacraments

1. May 27, 1525. Z IV:188–337.
2. Z IV:216:28–29.
3. Z IV:331:17–333:8.
4. November 5, 1525. Z IV:577–642.
5. November 6–8, 1525.
6. *Widerlegung der Ränke der Wiedertäufer.* July 31, 1527. Z VI/I:1–196.
7. Z VI/I:155–72.
8. Z VI/I:529–31.
9. Z VI/I:532–34.
10. Z XII:144:36–38; 144:39–145:1.
11. Z I:323:6–10.
12. Z I:460:6–7.
13. Z II:119:26–157:14.
14. Published in March 1525. Z III:322–54.
15. Z III:773–820.
16. *Nachhut wie Schlussschnörkel zum Abendmahl* Z IV:440–504.
17. Z IV:546–76.
18. Z IV:773–862.
19. See Locher, *Zwinglische Reformation*, 222.
20. Z III:228:19.
21. Stefan Niklaus Bosshard, *Zwingli-Erasmus-Cajetan. Die Eucharistie als Zeichen der Einheit* (Wiesbaden, 1978), 122.
22. E.g., Z III:534:1–4.
23. See below, pp. 146–48.
24. See Walther Köhler, ed., *Das Marburger Religionsegespräch 1529* (Leipzig, 1929).
25. Z VI/II:510–23.
26. *Notae Zwinglii. Randbemerkungen Zwinglis zu den Marburger Artikeln von 1529.* October 24, 1529. Z:VI/II:532–51. No other speech manuscript at all has been preserved, other than these Latin notes by Zwingli.
27. Bosshard, *Zwingli-Erasmus-Cajetan*, 96.
28. Z VI/II:806:6–12.

Chapter IX. Confession and Politics (1529–1531)

1. Before March 1530. Z VI/II:733–40.
2. "Erläuterung des christlichen Glaubens," July 1531. Z no. 181; S IV:44–78; HS II:295–394.
3. Analysis by Locher, *Zwingli*, 1982: 52–59.
4. "Rechenschaft des Glaubens," July 3, 1530. Z VI/II:753–817.
5. Z VII/II:792:6–10.

6. Z VI/II:815:21-23.

7. Fritz Blanke, Z VI/II:776.

8. July 14, 1530, to Luther. Hans Volz, ed., *Melanchthons Werke in Auswahl*, vol. 7, part 2 (Gütersloh, 1975): 216:22.

9. *Ad illustrissimos Germaniae princepes Augustae congregatos de convitiis Eccii epistola*, August 27, 1530. Z VI/III:231-91.

10. August 20, 1530. Z VI/III:1-230.

11. Z VI/III:57-62.

12. Johann Adam Möhler, Eduard Zeller, Alexander Schweizer.

13. Paul Wernle.

14. Wilhelm Dilthey, Reinhold Seeberg.

15. Locher, *Zwinglische Reformation*, 503.

16. Especially articles 1-5.

17. September 18, 1530, to Zwingli. Z XI:139:9-140:19.

18. Z VI/III:181:12-183:6.

19. Z VI/III:120:7-11.

20. February 12, 1531. Z XI:339-43.

21. Kurt Spillmann, *Zwingli und die zürcherische Politik gegenüber der Abtei St. Gallen* (St. Gallen, 1965), 13.

22. *Konzept zu einem Ratschlag der geheimen Räte für den Tag zu Zürich vom 10. bis 13. April 1531.* Z VI/IV: no. 173.

23. Helmut Meyer, *Der Zweite Kappeler Krieg* (Zurich, 1976), 49.

24. Ibid., 70.

25. Ibid., 77.

26. Ibid., 316-23.

Chapter X. Zwingli's Historical Impact

1. Regarding this concept, see Jacques Vincent Pollet, *Huldrych Zwingli et la Réforme en Swisse d'après les recherches récentes* (Paris, 1963), 93-98.

2. Locher, *Zwinglische Reformation*, 197-225.

3. Joachim Staedtke, "Bullingers Theologie—eine Fortsetzung der zwinglischen?" in Ulrich Gäbler and Endre Zsindely, eds., *Bullinger-Tagung 1975* (Zurich, 1977; reprint, 1982), 98.

4. Hans Ulrich Bächtold, *Bullinger vor dem Rat* (Bern and Frankfurt am Main, 1982), 15.

5. Carl Pestalozzi, *Heinrich Bullinger, Leben und ausgewählte Schriften* (Elberfeld, 1858), 88-91.

6. End of January/beginning of February 1532, to Bucer. *Heinrich Bullinger: Briefwechsel*, ed. Ulrich Gäbler et al. (Zurich, 1982), II:42-44.

7. *Chronika vom Leben und Wirken des Ulrich Zwingli*, ed. Leo Weisz (Zurich, 1932).

8. See the typology of Upper German city Reformation in Heiko Augustinus Oberman, *Werden und Wertung der Reformation. Vom Wegestreit zum Glaubenskampf* (Tübingen, 1977), 371-78.

9. See Locher, *Zwinglische Reformation*, 621–80.

10. Fritz Büsser, *Das katholische Zwinglibild* (Zurich and Stuttgart, 1968), 396.

11. Professor of church history in Zurich, 1893–1908.

12. Egli's successor until 1929.

13. "Zwingli," in *Die Religion in Geschichte und Gegenwart*, vol. 6 (Tübingen, 1962, 1968).

Chapter XI. Bibliographical Survey

1. Köhler, *Huldrych Zwingli*, in the introduction.

2. Zurich, 1943, 1946, 1954, 1960.

INDEX OF NAMES
AND PLACES

INDEX OF SUBJECTS

194